SINGLE-HANDED
Spey Casting

Solutions to Casts, Obstructions, Tight Spots,
and Other Casting Challenges of Real-Life Fishing

SIMON GAWESWORTH

STACKPOLE
BOOKS

Published by
STACKPOLE BOOKS
5067 Ritter Road
Mechanicsburg, PA 17055
www.stackpolebooks.com

Printed in China

First edition

10 9 8 7 6 5 4 3 2 1

Fly fishing can take people to the most remote and beautiful parts of the world, with clean rivers, lakes, and oceans. Please remember how important the environment is to your sport and help protect it. Do your bit. Reduce, reuse, and recycle. Reduce waste and water consumption. Reuse, rather than renew. Recycle, and buy things that are recyclable.

And remember, organic farms and farming practices do not put such toxic and harmful chemicals into the water system as modern commercial farming practices do. Support organic farming methods, please. Your sport will benefit from it.

Photographs by Jim Vincent; additional photos for chapter 24 by Kevin Bell
Illustrations by Greg Pearson

Mixed Sources

Product group from well-managed
forests, controlled sources and
recycled wood or fibre
www.fsc.org Cert no. SCS-COC-001907
© 1996 Forest Stewardship Council

FSC

This book was printed using responsible environmental practices by FSC-certified book manufacturers. The Forest Stewardship Council (FSC) encourages the responsible management of the world's forests.

Library of Congress Cataloging-in-Publication Data

Gawesworth, Simon.
  Single-handed spey casting : solutions to casts, obstructions, tight spots, and other casting challenges of real-life fishing / Simon Gawesworth. — 1st ed.
      p. cm.
  Includes index.
  ISBN-13: 978-0-8117-0559-2 (hardcover)
  ISBN-10: 0-8117-0559-5 (hardcover)
  1. Spey casting. I. Title.
  SH454.25.G378 2010
  799.12'4—dc22
                                    2009014646

To Susan, Chlöe, and Tristan,
still my universe

CONTENTS

Foreword   vi

Introduction   vii

SECTION 1. THE BASICS OF FLY CASTING   **1**

  1. The Basics   2

  2. Cast Groups   8

  3. The Forward Stroke   10

  4. The Catch Cast   13

SECTION 2. PROBLEMS BEHIND   **17**

  5. The Roll Cast   18

  6. Getting It Out!   28

  7. The Double Roll Cast   32

  8. The Switch Cast   35

  9. The Single Spey   47

  10. The Double Spey   68

  11. The Snake Roll   88

  12. The Snap T   100

  13. The Dry-Fly Spey   116

SECTION 3. PROBLEMS IN FRONT   **125**

  14. The Side Cast   126

  15. The Shepherd's Crook Cast   135

  16. The Reach Cast   144

  17. The Aerial Mend   149

  18. Slack-Line Casts   155

SECTION 4. COMBINED PROBLEMS   **161**

  19. The Roll Cast with Side Cut   162

  20. Spey Casts with Side Cut   171

  21. Sneaky Spey Casts   180

SECTION 5. ADDING DISTANCE   **191**

  22. Hauling   192

  23. Advanced D Loops   208

  24. The Joy of Slack (or Poking It)   215

  25. Turbo Casts   224

SECTION 6. TACKLE   **233**

  26. Rods   234

  27. Fly Lines   236

  28. Leaders   240

Glossary   242

Acknowledgments   244

Index   246

Fly fishing comprises many skills, but casting is the skill that alone defines it, regardless of venue or species. When an angler once asked me, "What makes a great casting coach?" I suggested three qualities: a thorough knowledge of the mechanics of casting; the ability to diagnose flaws in those mechanics in real time; the ability to explain clearly the caster's problem and recommend a remedy. Most instructors fall short in at least one category.

Years ago, while I was working as an editorial consultant on a comprehensive angling book for a London publisher, I knew Simon Gawesworth only as one name among dozens of contributors. Several years later I met him personally at a fly show in New Jersey. As I stood mesmerized, watching him perform his magic with a two-handed rod, I said to my wife, "I have to meet this guy." That first introduction established, and every subsequent meeting confirmed, my admiration for the man. His talent is prodigious, his knowledge awesome, his teaching ability rare. He makes complex concepts easy to grasp. Most importantly, he loves to share. He has no ego and never tries to impress you with what he can do.

Simon Gawesworth has had more positive impact on two-handed casting in the United States (within the sport and the industry) than any other person. For me, he is the standard by which all others should be judged. His first book, *Spey Casting* (Stackpole Books, 2004), made spey techniques with two-handed rods more understandable for salmon and steelhead anglers than any previous work. Despite its long tradition in the United Kingdom, Ireland, and Scandinavia, as well as decades of use by a cadre in the Pacific Northwest, too many American anglers viewed spey casting an unnecessary import. Few had knowledge of it or possessed the skill to use it. But the sport is changing. Every day, more anglers awaken to the potential of two-handed rods and, more important, to the techniques that, as this new work demonstrates, are applicable to one-handed rods as well.

There are countless more one-handed than two-handed rods in anglers' hands and, no doubt, always will be. That makes this new work a valuable and needed sequel to his first, and it de-serves to be in the hands of virtually every angler, whether fresh- or saltwater. Here, Simon shares his formidable knowledge of rod and line handling techniques that most anglers have seldom used, but certainly should. In transferring his ideas to the interests of one-handed casters, he dwells on practical, everyday situations in which we anglers find ourselves. He illustrates and reinforces his clear verbal descriptions of the techniques with excellent photographs and drawings, in a format similar to those that have made *Spey Casting* a classic. One of the strong points of *Single-Handed Spey Casting* is the emphasis on the advantages of learning to cast with either hand in order to accommodate various angling conditions. All this is done with an exactness of detail born of deep understanding and experience.

Even if you have never cast with a two-handed rod or have no intentions of doing so at present, learning the many useful casts that Simon presents will make the transition to two-handed rods simple, comfortable, and seamless, should you want to explore that world in the future. He follows explanations of traditional spey moves with modern refinements adapted to the needs of small stream anglers, particularly trout fishers. His presentations are as thorough as they are brilliant. For example, he carefully reviews traditional curve, reach, slack line casts, and aerial mends, before combining them with spey moves. This leads to a series of "Frankenstein" or "Heineken" casts. His tasteful tongue-in-cheek humor makes the going that much more enjoyable.

I was introduced to spey casting in England about 20 years ago, but this book jets my understanding of the techniques light years ahead. We imported the basics of fly fishing from England, but Simon Gawesworth may be our most valuable import in the centuries since. If you've not met him, watched him instruct or perform, nor studied his film or writings on spey casting, you are in for a rare treat. Be prepared to learn and have fun.

Ed Jaworowski
Chester Springs, Pennsylvania
July 2009

INTRODUCTION

Fly casting is a skill developed over time and with practice. Like any skill, it helps to have a good foundation on which to build, ensuring that the practice is worthy and not reinforcing bad habits and mistakes. However, fly fishing is a unique skill among sports, as the usual acceptance of the day's success is whether the angler caught a fish or not. In tennis, golf, even shooting (a close skill to angling), it is pretty obvious if your skill level is low; you can't keep the ball in the court or your driving is all over the place and you can't make a putt, or you miss the bird that flighted toward you. If a fly fisher is not catching fish, they can blame the fish: "they're not feeding today!" or "they are farther down the river." Of course, this can be true, but it can also be an excuse for the fly caster who cannot make a long enough cast to reach the fish or cope with a pool that is overgrown and tricky to fish.

Many years ago (in the good old days), I used to fish competitively in England; I fished local competitions, team competitions, club competitions, national championships, European championships, and world championships. I fished river competitions and lake competitions, and I enjoyed (and learned from) every one. However, I remember one of the first major competitions I fished. It was the final of the national river championships, and thirty-six anglers were competing to get in the top five so they could qualify to fish the home river international the following year. (The home international is between England, Scotland, Ireland, and Wales.) The day was divided into three sessions, and in each session competitors fished one of three different stretches of river (beats). The anglers were split into groups of twelve and competed against the eleven other anglers in the group, rotating to another beat every two hours with the same group. The chap who caught the most fish in session 1, group 1, would get 1 point, the angler who caught the second most in that group would get 2 points, and so on, with anyone catching nothing guaranteed last place (12 points, in this case). At the end of the day, an angler might have first place in session 1 (1 point), third place in session 2 (3 points), and second place (2 points) in the last session—totaling 6 points. The five people with the lowest score would fish for England the next year.

I did okay in my first session, catching a few fish—more than some, not as many as others—and picked up third place. In the second session I discovered that the beat my group was assigned to had lots of fast, open, skinny water with very little potential and one pool. The pool was ideal, with a shallow gravel bar running close to the near bank and a medium current flowing throughout the length. The pool varied between about six feet and eight feet in depth and was about fifty-five feet wide, with the odd overhanging tree on the far bank (where the current ran) providing cover for the trout. As I watched the pool I saw half a dozen noses poking out, feeding in the current seam, and rubbed my hands with glee. Easy pickings! With only about five feet of room behind me, I had to use a number of special casts to get the fly out to the fish, but they were pretty ready to take a fly when I got a cast out to them, and in the two hours, I landed eleven measurable fish. This was an easy first place. The third session was comparable to my first one with a few fish and second place. At the weigh-in at the end of the day, I found out I was the only person to have caught a fish in that deep pool on beat 2. Every other angler had either walked past the pool, assuming it was too difficult to fish, or made a few casts, lost a few flies and did not manage to reach the fish. The anglers had moved on to the shallower open water and struggled to find feeding fish. I ended up in the top 5 and with my first international cap!

Since that cap I have been fortunate enough to fish for England in many competitions: domestic competitions, home internationals, European championships, and world championships, and in the majority of these events, I have found tricks and casts that have helped me winkle out a fish or two.

Knowing some of the special ways of casting a fly can get you a fish in many tricky situations and turn a fishless day (or session) into a success.

The goal of this book is to open your eyes to the ways of casting a fly that can cope with obstructions behind you, in front of you, all around you, and make it easier for you to fish the waters that other anglers frustratingly walk by.

I hope you enjoy the read.

The English team at the 1999 world championship held in Australia. From left to right, top row: Ian (our guide), Andrew Ramsden, Chris Howitt, and Simon Gawesworth. Bottom row: Iain Barr, John Horsey, and Chris Ogborne.

THE BASICS
OF FLY CASTING

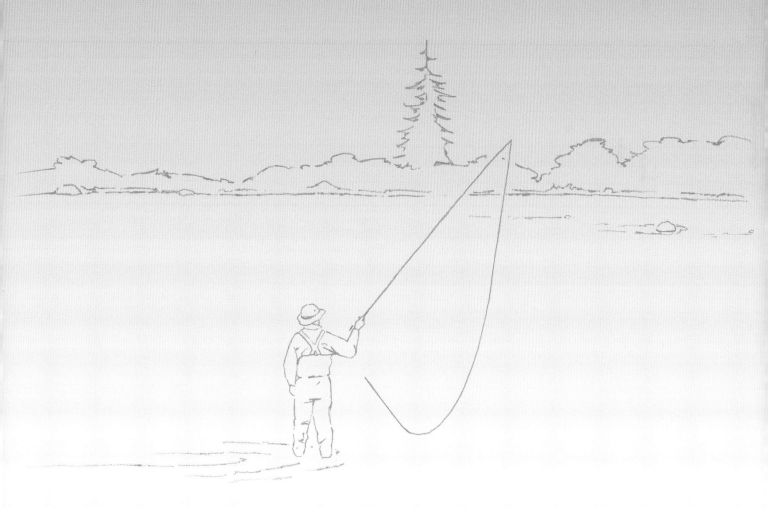

CHAPTER 1

The Basics

This book is not intended for the novice caster. An understanding and a degree of competence with the overhead cast is the minimum requirement to appreciate the following chapters. Nevertheless, many casters who know the overhead cast have little knowledge of how the thing works. Sure, you flick it back, you pause, you flick it forward, and it goes out there—somewhere. With practice, the "somewhere" becomes more controlled, and accuracy and distance increases. For the sake of filling in the blanks and for an understanding of the physics necessary to master the casts in this book, I'll start with two of the more basic facts that make the cast work, what I call "the two Ls"—load and loop.

Load

Flex

A fly rod is designed to flex, and it is this flex that should benefit the caster. At the very start, when making the backcast of a regular overhead cast, the rod flexes down toward the water as the rod is lifted and accelerated smoothly and continuously up and back (the loading move). Assuming the fly line is tight and straight on the water, the rod is bending (loading) against the grip the water has on the fly line combined with the weight of the fly line outside the rod. At the critical moment of the backstroke, the caster changes the nature of the load by snapping the wrist back and making a positive stop of the rod (the power arc). The wrist snap releases the built-up energy (flex) in the rod and transmits it into the fly line, while the positive stop of the rod ensures that the energy transfer is fast and efficient. It also helps control the size and shape of the loop as we shall see shortly.

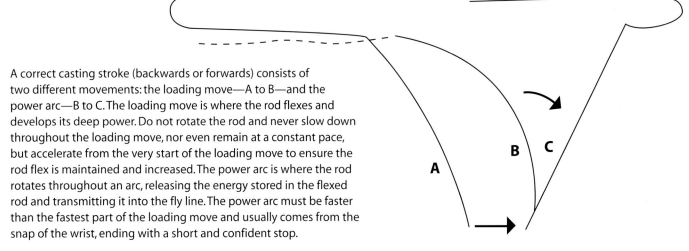

A correct casting stroke (backwards or forwards) consists of two different movements: the loading move—A to B—and the power arc—B to C. The loading move is where the rod flexes and develops its deep power. Do not rotate the rod and never slow down throughout the loading move, nor even remain at a constant pace, but accelerate from the very start of the loading move to ensure the rod flex is maintained and increased. The power arc is where the rod rotates throughout an arc, releasing the energy stored in the flexed rod and transmitting it into the fly line. The power arc must be faster than the fastest part of the loading move and usually comes from the snap of the wrist, ending with a short and confident stop.

With a properly executed backcast, you have enough speed to ensure the line unrolls completely in the air and straightens out. If you have thirty feet of line outside the rod (including the leader), you need enough energy to make the fly travel more than thirty feet behind. (If you had just enough energy for the fly to travel the thirty feet, it would start to lose momentum and fall as the inertia ran out.) If casting with sixty feet of line, you need enough energy for the fly to go back more than sixty feet, and so on.

At this stage of the cast, and at the very start of the forward cast, we have an interesting derivation of rod flex. The rod flexes from three separate loads: 1) the slight pull of the fly line as it travels backwards, 2) the weight of the line as the rod drives against it, and 3) the air resistance against the rod thickness (and, though to a lesser extent, the line surface).

I see no need to get into the subtleties of the load achieved by the pull of the line or of the air resistance on the rod and line in this book. Instead, I want to concentrate on where the majority of the load comes from—the weight of the line behind the rod. In simple terms, the caster making a thirty-foot backcast has less line weight to load the rod than the caster making the sixty-foot cast, so the rod will have less flex as it is driven forward. This is fine for a short cast, but for distance you will need more than a loaded rod tip to help and, if the rod won't give you the entire load, the effort must come from you. In other words, your work effort will need to increase.

Leverage

The rod is a lever. A longer rod will generate more line speed throughout the power arc (rotation) than a shorter rod—assuming the lever is not so long that it requires too much effort to rotate it. This is easily demonstrated with a simple picture (see bottom diagram).

During the rod's rotation, the longer lever will travel faster. However, when driving a rod forward with no rotation (prior to the power arc), a longer lever will travel at the same speed as the shorter one.

I mention the leverage aspect at this stage only to illustrate that it is part of line speed, load, and distance, but in reality no one is going to change the length of the lever in midcast.

An aside note is that two rods of the same length don't necessarily have the same leverage. If you took a nine-foot rod that was very fast and a nine-foot rod that was very soft and slow and you loaded them up with identical line weight and length, the fast rod would actually be a longer lever. My dad, who was a teacher of math and physics before he became a fly-fishing instructor, showed me this one day while trying to give me an understanding of fly casting. The easiest way to see this is through the illustration on page 4.

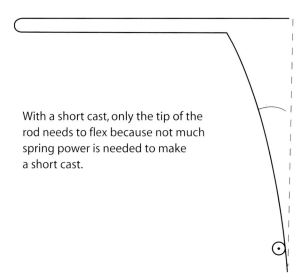

With a short cast, only the tip of the rod needs to flex because not much spring power is needed to make a short cast.

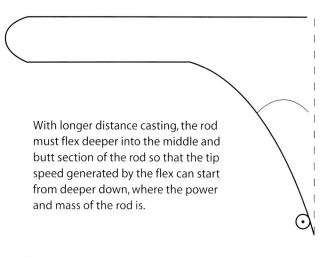

With longer distance casting, the rod must flex deeper into the middle and butt section of the rod so that the tip speed generated by the flex can start from deeper down, where the power and mass of the rod is.

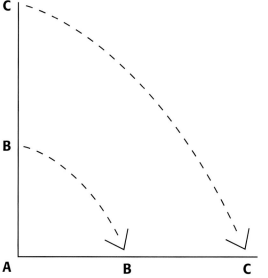

In this diagram, you have a solid lever (not flexing like a fly rod). If point A is stationary and the lever rotates through ninety degrees in one second, point A has traveled basically zero inches in one second. Point B, some way up the lever, might travel two feet in that one second, whereas point C, at the very end of the lever, could travel as much as six feet in the same time, thus traveling faster.

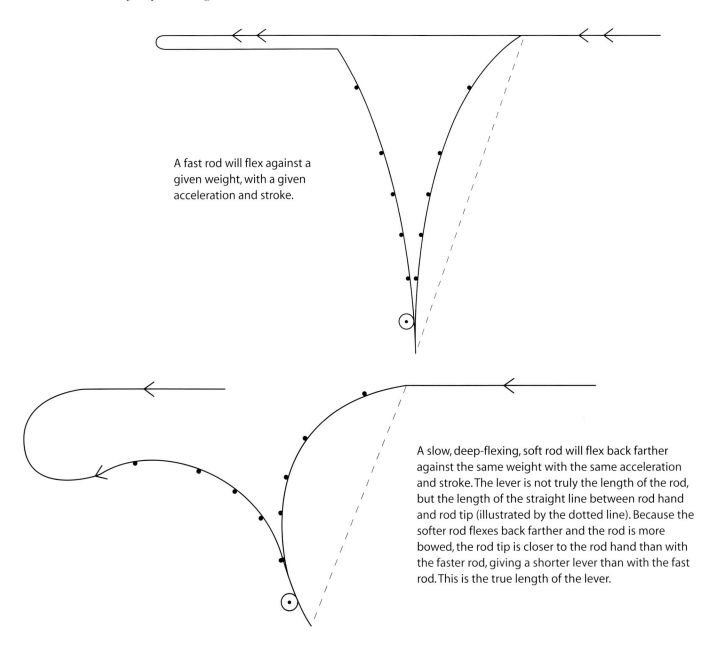

A fast rod will flex against a given weight, with a given acceleration and stroke.

A slow, deep-flexing, soft rod will flex back farther against the same weight with the same acceleration and stroke. The lever is not truly the length of the rod, but the length of the straight line between rod hand and rod tip (illustrated by the dotted line). Because the softer rod flexes back farther and the rod is more bowed, the rod tip is closer to the rod hand than with the faster rod, giving a shorter lever than with the fast rod. This is the true length of the lever.

Acceleration

As mentioned above, acceleration is critical to increase the load in a casting stroke. As long as the rod accelerates during the loading move and finishes with a slightly faster power arc, the cast will be effective. Other factors, such as loop size, rod action, line size, leader/fly combination, and weather conditions influence how effective the acceleration is, but if you can remember to keep a smooth, constant acceleration throughout a casting stroke, you will have a solid foundation on which all fly casts can be built.

A lot of fly-casting instructors use the phrase "long line, long stroke; short line, short stroke," and the simplicity of this statement should not be forgotten. The main reason for this statement is obvious. If a caster has a loading move of six inches prior to the power arc, very little flex will be put into the rod, leaving little possibility of reaching a high speed through six inches of acceleration. If the same caster has a loading move of four feet, the rod will flex much farther down (storing more energy), and the length of the acceleration will generate a higher speed at the end of the stroke. The end result, obviously, is that the long stroke gives a much greater load into the rod and, therefore, more distance.

Acceleration comes from many parts of the body. It should come from the arm, the wrist, the shoulder, through body rotation and the transfer of body weight/mass during the casting stroke. Simply put, it comes from you—the caster—and you should never forget how important acceleration is to a casting stroke.

Many years ago, when I was doing the demonstration circuit of fly-fishing shows in the UK, I had a routine that showed it was possible to cast without any rod flex. I took my old pool cue and whipped a couple of rod rings (one at the tip) and a reel seat on it. During the demos I would cast a WF7 fly line with this cue. I could cast it fifty feet or so, but it took effort to do this as there was no flex in the cue to help. The pool cue was five feet long, so the only way I could generate any line speed to make a cast was

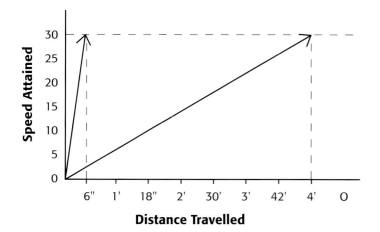

Distance Travelled

Let's look at two examples of acceleration. For the sake of simple math, assume that it takes thirty units (miles per hour, inches per second … whatever) to generate enough speed to make a twenty-five-foot cast. With only six inches of travel, the acceleration would have to be incredibly violent and sudden to get to that speed from a standing start in such a short distance. Over a length of four feet, it can be much smoother and more controlled—more efficient. We are, or should be, all about efficient casting techniques.

to utilize arm and wrist speed and the five-foot length of leverage to basically throw out the fly line. I could throw a very tight loop but had to really work at getting the cast to go any distance.

Another part of the demonstration was to put the pool cue down and thread the fly line through a one-inch split ring. I cupped the split ring in my right thumb and index finger and proceeded to cast with only my hand, arm, and wrist. Again, there is no flex or spring power when casting this way, and I had negated the five-foot length of leverage. This shows that it is possible to cast without any flex or leverage length and that the power only came from my arm and wrist speed. However, it could never be called efficient!

If you break the amount of power applied in a casting stroke into two parts—rod power and caster power—you will have a ratio. I call this the energy ratio. The ratio is simple: If the rod contributes 70 percent of the power needed to make the cast, the caster needs to add 30 percent of power. This is mostly through the amount of acceleration and energy imparted by the shoulder, arm, and wrist. If the rod only contributes 10 percent of the power, the caster is going to have to work much harder to get the same result. In my demonstration with the pool cue, I would have had some contribution just through the length of the lever; however, in the split ring demonstration, I had no assistance from a rod, so I had to apply 100 percent of the power.

Loop

The shape the fly line takes at the end of each casting stroke is called a loop. Like people, loops come in all different shapes and sizes, and there isn't a perfect loop for every situation. Good casters can control their loop size and shape according to the fishing requirements. In almost every situation, the loop needs to unroll fully and straighten out, with just enough power to make that happen. Too much power is a waste of energy and can result in a savage kick of the line. Too little power and the loop fails to unroll and will collapse on itself.

The shape and size of the loop is controlled by the path of the rod tip, the rod action, the stop at the end of each stroke, and the acceleration throughout the entire stroke. As I mentioned earlier, this book isn't going to cover the overhead cast and its intricacies as there are plenty of great books on this subject.

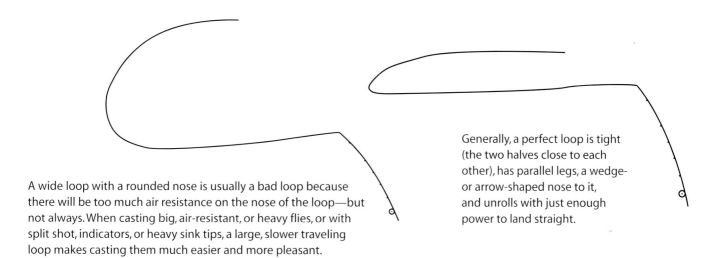

A wide loop with a rounded nose is usually a bad loop because there will be too much air resistance on the nose of the loop—but not always. When casting big, air-resistant, or heavy flies, or with split shot, indicators, or heavy sink tips, a large, slower traveling loop makes casting them much easier and more pleasant.

Generally, a perfect loop is tight (the two halves close to each other), has parallel legs, a wedge- or arrow-shaped nose to it, and unrolls with just enough power to land straight.

However, for some of the casts I talk about later on, I believe it is necessary to outline some basics on loop formation.

We've already looked at the part of the casting stroke I call the power arc. One other thing about this power arc is that it is the foundation of the size of the loop. During the loading move, the rod can travel in quite an arc, but for a tight loop, the power arc must be contained and, actually, form not so much of an arc. The rod tip, during this vital stage of the cast, needs to travel in a straight line and finish with a stop that is both decisive and firm. The straight line can be in any plane—vertical, horizontal, or tilted at any angle in between—but straight and true it must travel.

Conversely, to make a larger, rounded loop, the rod tip arc should be opened up and the straight line path ignored. You can do this by using a softer, deep-flexing rod for the situations that need these wider loops, or you can just do it by slowing down the casting stroke, hinging your wrist more throughout the power arc, and softening the stop.

The final part of the loop's role in this book is the turnover. A loop can only turn over (unroll from the elongated U shape to a straight horizontal line) if the bottom part of the loop travels slower than the top. This allows the top half of the loop to overtake the bottom half and unroll. If the bottom half were to travel at the same speed as the top half, there would never be any overtaking, unrolling, or turnover. The line would just run out of energy and collapse.

As you will see later in this book, there are casts that use the two Ls in more ways, and I will refer back to these pages as a reminder at each key point or cast.

The direct relationship

One thing I like my students to understand is the direct relationship between the load and the loop. As casters get better, they strive for the narrowest, tightest loops. Catalogs, brochures, and ads by professional fly-fishing companies show casters with tiny loops. They're like supermodels—the thinner and tighter they are, the sexier they are! There's even a web site (an excellent one, at that) dedicated to the best in casting tips and techniques called Sexy Loops.

The bottom line in casting circles is that the better casters are, the tighter the loops they want to cast. Bigger is not better here.

The reason I mention this is that I want to finish this chapter by stating that the more power a caster puts into a fly rod, the bigger the loop will tend to be. Any caster with a bit of experience can cast a loop three inches wide with only six feet of fly line outside the rod tip. You make tiny little rod tip twitches, and the line will form a deliciously small loop, but with little line speed. To do it with a long line takes a lot more ability. Try casting seventy feet of line with only the same tiny rod tip twitches! You can, if the rod loads from the fly line, but you can't if the rod loads from a caster's power. Get an energy ratio of 90 percent line load and 10 percent caster's effort, and you can get the sexiest loops in the world!

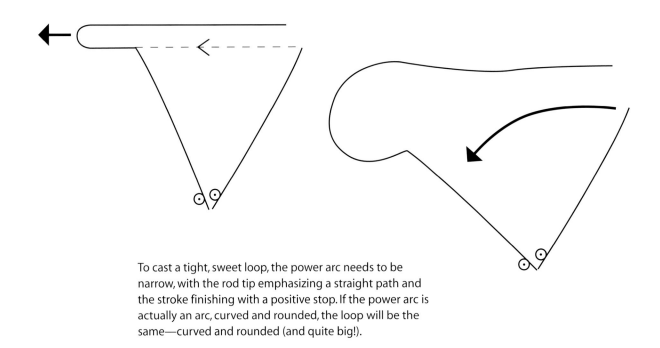

To cast a tight, sweet loop, the power arc needs to be narrow, with the rod tip emphasizing a straight path and the stroke finishing with a positive stop. If the power arc is actually an arc, curved and rounded, the loop will be the same—curved and rounded (and quite big!).

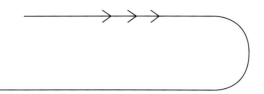

When making a forward cast and forming a loop, a certain amount of speed is imparted into the loop. For the sake of simplicity in the following diagrams, I am going to give this a unit of speed of thirty. If you make a cast and hold the line tight, shooting none at all, the top half of the loop has a speed of thirty and the bottom half of the loop, anchored because you are not shooting line, doesn't move, which equals zero. This gives an overtaking speed of thirty, which is very positive.

When releasing line on the forward cast, the bottom half of the loop now travels away from you as well. With a thick fly line like a double taper, there is enough friction and drag on the fly line as it shoots through the rod rings to slow the bottom half of the loop down—in this example by twenty units. The top half of the loop still travels at thirty units, but the bottom half is effectively only traveling at ten units, which gives an overtaking speed of twenty—still plenty for a good loop turnover.

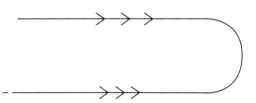

If you use a super thin shooting line with a shooting head, like a hard, slick nylon with a narrow diameter, and release line for distance, the friction and drag of the thin line going through the rod rings is greatly reduced. This results in more distance in the shoot but often a collapsed forward cast and lack of turnover. Using the same example as the others, the top half of the loop still travels at thirty, whereas the bottom (with only five units of friction) now travels at twenty-five, giving an overtaking speed of just five. Not enough to get great turnover or presentation!

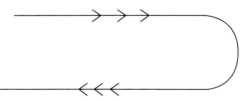

If, instead of shooting the line on the forward cast, you actually tug the line backwards with the tip of the rod, or give a pull to the line near the stripping guide, the effect would be very different. The top half would still travel at thirty, but if you tugged at thirty, you would have an overtaking speed of sixty—the greatest of all. Many good casters use this technique when they see their forward cast running out of steam and about to collapse. A sharp tug of the line or a twitch or lift with the rod tip can suddenly reverse this collapsing cast and make the line kick over and present perfectly. Be careful when executing this because too hard a tug, or tugging at all when there is plenty of turnover speed anyway, will result in a savage lash over of the line tip and leader and a nasty crash and dump onto the water.

CHAPTER 2

Cast Groups

With so many casts to cover in this book and numerous principles that apply to some casts and not others, I think it is a good idea to describe the main groups that the casts fall into. The reason for this is simple: a number of principles apply to a group of casts, and if you know the principles of a group, it saves having to learn the same principles for every cast within that group. If you remember the principles of a group of casts and all the casts within that group have the same principles, each cast becomes less difficult to understand.

At this stage I don't expect that sentence to mean much, but it will as you read through this book.

To-and-Fro Casts

There are two simple cast groups. The group of casts known as the to-and-fro casts are the regular casts like the overhead cast, the pick-up-and-lay-down cast, and the side cast. These casts have a backcast that forms above the rod tip and fully unrolls to a straight line before the forward cast starts. These casts should rarely touch the water on the backcast.

The to-and-fro casts form a regular-shaped loop above the rod tip that extends fully behind you before the forward cast starts. The backcast should not touch the water.

Continuous Motion Casts

The continuous motion casts all have backcasts that form underneath the rod tip, which never straightens out behind you and always anchors (touches) the water.

My dad taught me how to fly-cast, fly-fish, and teach many years ago. I was lucky to grow up with a dad who had a fly-fishing school. I learned the right way to cast from an early age and didn't develop too many bad habits. My dad named many of the techniques and terminologies that are used today, and the continuous motion cast is one of his. He gave this name to all casts that don't have a backcast that unrolls fully behind the caster—casts such as the roll cast, the spey casts, and many of the casts I am going to examine in this book. The main thing to remember about the continuous motion casts is that these casts have a backcast that forms *underneath* the rod tip, never extends fully behind you, and always anchors on the water.

Within the continuous motion casts are two groups, what I call the airborne anchor and the waterborne anchor casts. Later on you will see the significance of splitting this group into two subgroups and you'll learn which casts fall into which group.

Airborne Anchor vs. Waterborne Anchor Casts

Most of the continuous motion casts have either two rod strokes (movements) or three rod strokes to complete the cast. There will always be a forward stroke to get the line in front and out to the fish. There is also always a stroke called the D-loop stroke. This is basically the backcast—the stroke that forms a thing called a D loop underneath the rod tip and anchored on the water. The third stroke that is part of some of the continuous motion casts is called the setup stroke. This basically sets the line into a position to make the D-loop stroke easier or more effective.

More on these strokes later, but I do want to briefly mention the D-loop stroke. Strange as it may sound (at this stage of the book), when you make a D-loop stroke, you can either have the line in the air throughout the stroke or the line on the water during the entire stroke.

Any cast that has the fly line traveling through the air during the D-loop stroke is classified as an airborne anchor cast. Casts with a D-loop stroke where the line remains on the water throughout the whole stroke are called waterborne anchor casts.

As I said earlier, the reason for knowing about the cast groups is that many of the basic principles and physics of the casts within a single group are very similar. As you read through each chapter, you will see the relevance of this, and I will refer to the four groups—to and fro, continuous motion and its subgroups, airborne anchor and waterborne anchor, in each chapter.

If the line remains on the water during the D-loop stroke, that cast is part of the waterborne anchor subgroup.

If, during any of the continuous motion casts, the fly line travels back through the air during the backcast (the D-loop stroke) and then touches the water, that cast is part of the airborne anchor subgroup.

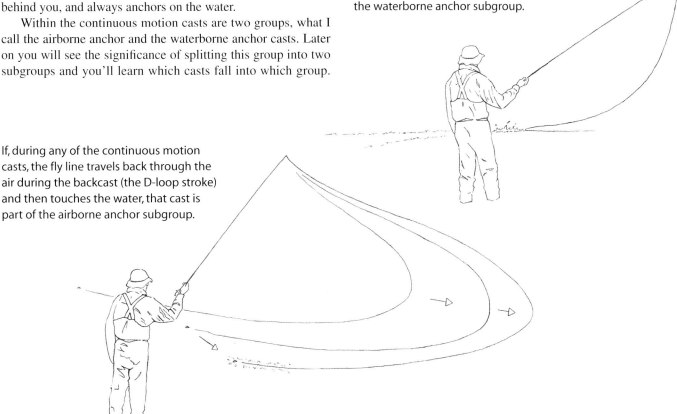

CHAPTER 3

The Forward Stroke

This book developed into a bigger project than I had ever intended. (Why did I not hark back to the words I said after I had written my first book, *Spey Casting*, namely, "I'll never write another book again!"?) These things have a habit of growing out of control, and my original intention was to write a book solely on spey-casting techniques for the single-handed rod. However, as I started to write the book, I found big glaring gaps in what I was writing, and I had to take a step or two back. I figure that if you know the basics, you can move on and not read what I have to write about them. If you are starting, then I would hate to baffle you (even more) by leaving out some basic information. So the project grew, the book grew, and this chapter evolved!

It may seem strange to start with what is actually the last part of the cast, but if you can get a good solid forward stroke dialed in to a point where there is little or no thought required, it is a good thing. A lot of the theory and techniques for the forward stroke are mirrored on the backstroke anyway, and it is

easier to start with one thing than to try and remember to focus on several things at the same time. A cast examined later (and one that many casters know, to an extent anyway) called the roll cast has no backcast at all and is a useful cast for teaching or learning the correct development of the forward stroke—but I am getting ahead of myself here.

Of particular relevance is the section of this book titled Problems Behind. If there is an obstacle behind you, you would be pretty daft to make a backcast, so most casts in that section have no backcast. They are all continuous motion casts, and as you read through the book, I hope you will start to see that all there is to these continuous motion casts is the correct positioning of the fly line on the water (the anchor) followed by a good forward stroke. You might drag, flick, flop, snap, poke, collapse, or steer the line into the correct position (or a combination of these), but the one binding factor of all these casts is a good forward delivery. So let's nail it here.

The ABCs

My dad always used to tell me "there is no such thing as a stupid student, only a stupid teacher." He believed that there was always a phrase, analogy, visual image, or prop of some kind that would ring the bell with students and help them see the picture, no matter what (or who) had failed in the past. As a result, a lot of my teaching techniques—both in classes and in writing—contain analogies. The analogy I have found the most useful that gives the clearest picture for the forward cast is the ABC.

Each forward cast (and backcast, for that matter) has to have a certain movement, rod path, power application, transfer of power, and stop of the rod to succeed. Of these, the biggest factor influencing the success of the casting stroke is the change of power. When you make a backcast, your hand, arm, and rod are in the key position, usually with the rod around 1 o'clock and the hand level with the ear.

The forward casting stroke should start from this key position with a loading move, a move of the hand, arm, shoulder, body, rod, or whatever, that makes the rod flex backwards. The flex is the load. Following the loading move is the power arc or stroke, which terminates with the release of the load and the energy built up in the rod.

I call the loading move AB, where A is the rod's position at the start of the casting stroke, with little or no load, and B is where the rod stops loading and starts to arc. The power arc or stroke is BC, B being the same—the stop of the load and the start of the power—and C being the stop of the power. (See the diagram.)

The reason I like to use the ABC analogy is that it gives a caster a very clear idea of the change in the casting stroke and where it takes place. It is also a useful tool in future lessons. The length of AB is not always the same. For a number of reasons (which I will go into throughout this book), the AB could vary in length from a six-inch movement to a full forty inches.

Before we move on from the ABCs, I want to reinforce a vital point: In all cases, regardless of how long the AB is, the rod does not rotate until it reaches B and never slows down. The rod should always accelerate throughout the length of AB and then finish with a faster BC.

The correct hand position for the majority of casts is called the key position. The rod hand is about level with the ear, elbow bent and relaxed, and wrist open slightly. The rod should be at an angle of about 30 degrees past the vertical. Looking at it from this position, the rod is pointing to 11 o'clock. From the caster's perspective, this is 1 o'clock.

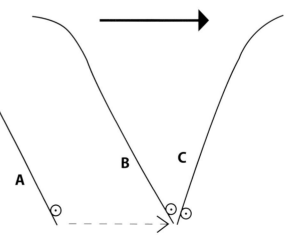

If you look at the rod casting stroke as a simple diagram, you can see that the rod starts the forward cast at position A. The rod loads as it drives through to position B without rotating. Throughout the entire length of the AB stroke, the rod travels at a set angle. When the rod reaches B, the forward drive comes to an end and the power arc snaps the rod over, rotating the rod to its stopping point at C.

Flex

To keep a cast efficient, one needs to enhance the load of the rod and use the natural flex to its maximum. This is easily done if you aim your forward cast directly opposite your backcast. Think of a bow and arrow, or a catapult, drawn back and ready to fire. Naturally the arrow or the stone will fire in a direction exactly opposite the pull. A rod should be treated the same. If you send a backcast due north, you should aim the forward cast due south. This is not always possible, especially when making a change of direction cast, but the more aligned the two casts are, the better the end result and the more efficient the cast will be. Not only should the forward cast be opposite the backcast in angle, but trajectory as well, if you want the very best and efficient forward cast.

When I was starting my fly-casting instruction life, I read a book by the late Hugh Falkus. One of the casts he described was called the steeple cast. The idea of the cast is to send a type of overhead cast up almost vertically in the air on the backcast and then straight out in front of you on the forward cast—ideal for when bushes are behind you. I tried this cast so many times, following all of the advice and techniques in the book, but could

never get the forward cast to do anything other than crash in a heap in front of me! Nowadays I understand the physics of the rod load, and if you can ever get a backcast climbing almost vertically above you, then the subsequent forward cast, driving almost vertically down, will drill a nice hole in the water in front of you!

Later on, as I go into the details of individual casts, I will try and make it a little more obvious how to align back- and forward casts when making a change of direction cast, but at this early stage of the basics, just know how important it is to work with the natural rod flex.

In summary, to get a really good forward cast, you need to maintain the ABCs of acceleration and rotation and drive the forward cast directly opposite the load. In the previous chapter on the basics, I described the load of the backcast, which creates enough flex to get the rod to do the necessary work forward, as well as the loop shape created by the straight line path of the rod tip and the positive forward stop—what a lot of things to remember, and we haven't even gotten to the casts themselves!

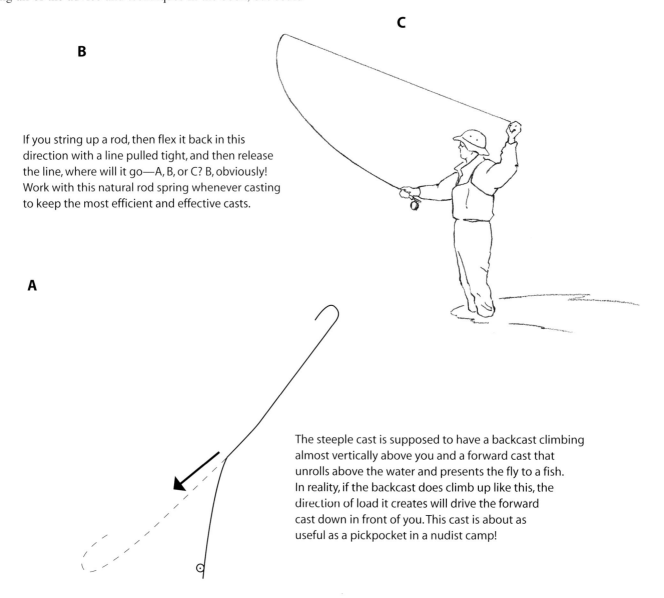

If you string up a rod, then flex it back in this direction with a line pulled tight, and then release the line, where will it go—A, B, or C? B, obviously! Work with this natural rod spring whenever casting to keep the most efficient and effective casts.

The steeple cast is supposed to have a backcast climbing almost vertically above you and a forward cast that unrolls above the water and presents the fly to a fish. In reality, if the backcast does climb up like this, the direction of load it creates will drive the forward cast down in front of you. This cast is about as useful as a pickpocket in a nudist camp!

CHAPTER 4

The Catch Cast

To-and-Fro Group

I want to start the actual casting part of this book with something a little unexpected, a cast I use a lot and love.

I use the catch cast countless times a day when fishing to change my fly, recoat a dry fly with floatant, pull weeds off the hook, examine my fly, check for knots, and more. It's not really a cast, just a way of getting the fly to your hand quickly. Remember, you can only catch a fish when your fly is in the water. If you hook some

When to use this cast: Anytime you need to check your fly, change your fly, or undo a tangle.

weed and want to get it off quickly, don't spend the time to strip the fly back to you, take the weed off, and then make four or five casts to get the fly back to where it was. Likewise, if you need to change your fly, why strip it in, change the fly, and then cast it back out? The catch cast saves these steps and ensures your fly is in hand very quickly indeed.

The following photos illustrate this technique.

Start the catch cast with your rod tip low, pointing at the fly, and the fly line lying straight on the water. Assuming you are right-handed, keep the rod in the right hand and hold your left hand out to the side. (Switch hands if you are a left-handed caster.)

Smoothly lift the rod tip up in a vertical plane, while still pointing in the direction of the fly line. Raise the rod to about 45 degrees, and accelerate slightly (but smoothly) to an angle of about 70 degrees.

Without any pause or reduction in rod speed, start to snap the rod tip downwards. This will put a slight S shape in the rod. Don't worry, this is fine!

Finish the downward snap abruptly and close to the water. This will snap the fly line out of the water and form a loop that travels toward you.

The loop should unroll toward you with the tip of the fly line, leader, and fly high in the air.

Watch the line tip as it falls toward your left hand.

As the line tip drops into your hand, close your hand and make the catch.

The cast is easy to learn and perform and very cool to watch. In my earlier demonstration days in England, I used to finish my demonstrations with a catch cast, sometimes catching as in the photos above, sometimes putting my left hand behind my back and catching it backhanded, and sometimes quickly changing hands, flipping the rod into my left hand while the loop traveled back to me, and catching the line in my right . . . just fancy showmanship stuff, but people loved it.

The only thing I will add here is how to aim the loop so it travels toward your left hand. Assuming there is no wind, if you make a vertical lift of the rod and a vertical snap down of it, you will land the line directly on your head—probably right between your eyes! If you don't want that and prefer the line to land in

your hand on the left side, just angle your rod about 5 degrees to the left before the initial lift. Keep the rod angled 5 degrees throughout the lift and the snap down, and the line should land in your hand. If 5 degrees doesn't work, try 8 degrees, 3 degrees, or whatever it takes until you can make the line land in your hand.

If you want to be a showman and make the backhanded catch I described above, just angle your rod about 2 degrees to the right for both the lift and the snap.

If you are trying this for the first time, do it a few times without a fly on, just in case your aim is poor. Get used to the technique and learn how to aim before trying the cast while out fishing with a fly on.

PROBLEMS BEHIND

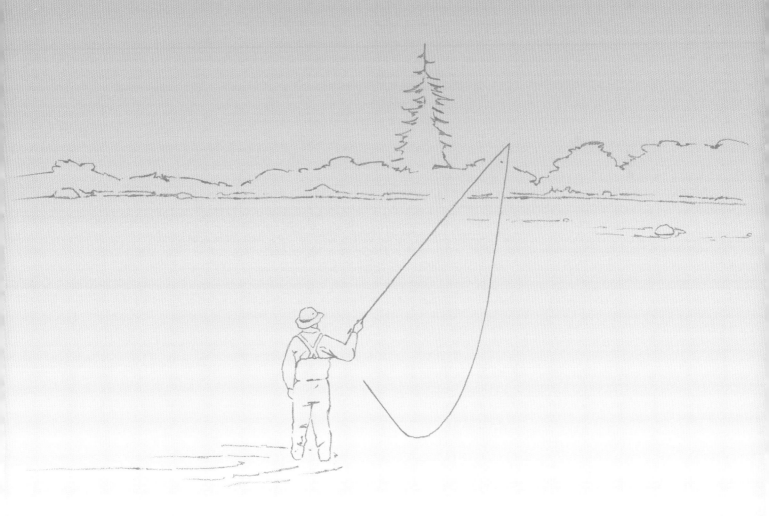

CHAPTER 5

The Roll Cast

Continuous Motion Group
Waterborne Anchor Subgroup

The first of the true casts I am going to examine is the roll cast. It is a cast that pretty much all moderate ability (and better) fly casters know, or think they know, how to do. However, in my experience, few of the casters I see fishing with a roll cast know what makes it work. It is no more than a means to an end for them, a way to get the fly out to the fish when there is an obstruction behind.

I am an instructor and a caster, and to me every cast is more than a means to an end. I enjoy casting and understanding how a

When to use this cast: no change of direction, obstructions behind, short to mid-distance, straightening out slack in the line, lifting sinking tips to the surface, casting large flies.

cast works, and I work to improve each cast, both for me and the people I teach. Nobody should be satisfied with a roll cast that rolls along the water with a wide, circular loop and collapses in slack—unless that is what you are trying to do. A good roll cast is like a good overhead cast: it unrolls in the air with a narrow loop, allowing the fly and all the fly line to land softly and at the same time.

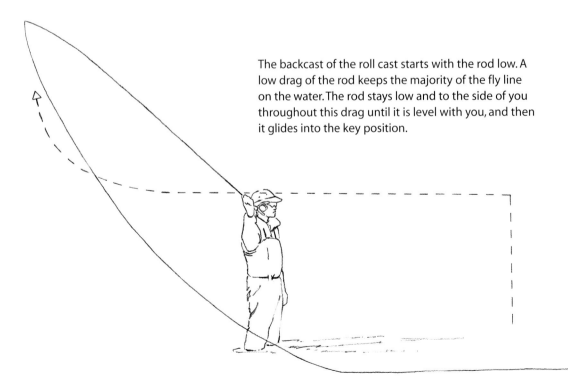

The backcast of the roll cast starts with the rod low. A low drag of the rod keeps the majority of the fly line on the water. The rod stays low and to the side of you throughout this drag until it is level with you, and then it glides into the key position.

18

A typical roll cast, as described and taught by many instructors in books and films, has a rounded loop.

This typical roll cast is wide and unrolls along the water, with your fly line landing first and your fly last.

In reality, a good roll cast should have a narrow loop that unrolls in the air and ensures that the fly and line land as one.

Let's take a look at the reasons for making a roll cast. The roll cast has one very simple benefit: no backcast. As a result, the roll cast can be used in many situations.

1. The most obvious one, and the one almost all fly casters use the roll cast for, is when there are obstructions behind, preventing a regular overhead cast.
2. With no backcast, it is also a useful tool when there is a load of slack line lying in the water in front. A backcast would fail because the slack line would never get the rod to load. A roll cast will straighten the line for a good overhead cast.
3. If you are fishing a deeply sunken line and need to make a cast without stripping the line in, a roll cast can bring the line up to the surface (you may need two or three for a long and really deeply sunk line) before you make the overhead cast.
4. Certain fishing techniques, such as traditional loch-style dibbling or when fishing spiders (soft hackles) upstream in a river, require the rod to be lifted as part of the technique. If the rod is lifted to the vertical, you have nothing left to make a backcast, so a roll cast gets the line in front and the rod down to a casting position—then you can make an overhead cast.
5. When making an overhead cast with big or heavy flies, they frequently kick at the end of the casting stroke when the loop is almost completely unrolled, prior to the start of the next casting stroke. Because the flies stay in the water during the backstroke (the D-loop stroke) of a roll cast, they cannot kick. So the roll cast is an excellent way to cast big, ungainly flies.

Despite this list, the first reason, obstructions behind, will still be the main reason for using the roll cast.

The roll cast starts with the rod and line in front of you, ideally with the rod tip low and the line straight (the roll cast is the only cast where this does not have to be the case). The backcast is no more than a drag of the line, not a cast as such. In a perfect roll cast, you drag the line back with the line, leader, and fly staying on the water during the entire backcast (D-loop stroke). This puts the cast into the waterborne anchor subgroup. Keep the rod tip low and out to the side throughout most of the drag until the rod reaches a point level with you, and then raise the rod to an angle of about 30 degrees beyond the vertical (also called 1 o'clock). At this stage, your elbow should remain bent and low, tucked in close to the side of your body. Your wrist should be cocked open slightly and around ear level—this is called the key position.

Most forward casts should start from this key position, with the elbow bent and low, the hand about ear level, and the wrist cocked open slightly, holding the rod at an angle of about 30 degrees past the vertical, or between 1 o'clock and 1:30 from the caster's aspect.

The D Loop

Once you are in the key position, there are a couple of basic things to know about the roll cast. The first is that with virtually no backcast you have virtually no line weight behind to load the rod. As I mentioned in the previous chapter, when you make an overhead cast, the backcast is what gives you a good load to flex the rod for the forward cast. So, if there is no backcast, what loads the rod? In truth, some line is behind the rod, though it is not cast there. It hangs from the rod in a curve called the D loop, which is what makes the rod load.

As you begin to understand the value of this D loop, you begin to appreciate that the size of the D loop affects the efficiency of the roll cast. The bigger the D loop is, the more efficient the resulting forward cast will be. Efficient means three things as far as a cast goes:

1. It can mean using less effort on the final cast to get the line out the required distance.
2. It can mean more distance for the same effort used for the less efficient cast.
3. It can mean tighter and sweeter loops—something all good casters strive to get!

When making a roll cast, most people are content to drag the rod level with their shoulder and then drive the forward cast out. However, a better way to load the rod is to extend the rod back farther with the arm, creating a deeper curve, or D loop, in the line. This will ensure that there is more weight to load the rod and make the roll cast more efficient.

You can also improve your technique by angling the rod farther back than the standard 1 o'clock position. However, this can add problems to the cast that negate the increased load, which I'll come to shortly.

In a roll cast, the line hangs from the rod in a curve called the D loop. The D loop provides the weight to flex the rod against for the forward cast.

When you drag your arm to your shoulder, a short movement, the D loop is small and hardly behind the rod at all. In this case it provides little load to assist the rod.

If you push your arm back behind your head a little before the forward cast, the D loop will be larger and the extra weight of the line will create more flex and load in the rod and provide a better cast.

The Rail Tracks

The other key thing to know with the roll cast is where you should aim the forward cast. A mate of mine and an excellent caster and instructor, Andy Murray, coined the phrase "the rail track" for teaching this fundamental principle. I think it gives a very clear picture of what one is trying to do, so I stole the term!

For the most effective roll cast, the forward stroke must be made as close to, and parallel to, the line that is lying on the water in front. Imagine two rail tracks going on toward the horizon, always parallel and always close. This is how your roll cast forward stroke should be. Call the fly line lying on the water in front of you one rail track. The other rail track is where you should aim your forward cast—close and parallel to the first.

One thing to remember at this stage of the game is that the roll cast is not a change of direction cast at all—not if you want to make an efficient cast.

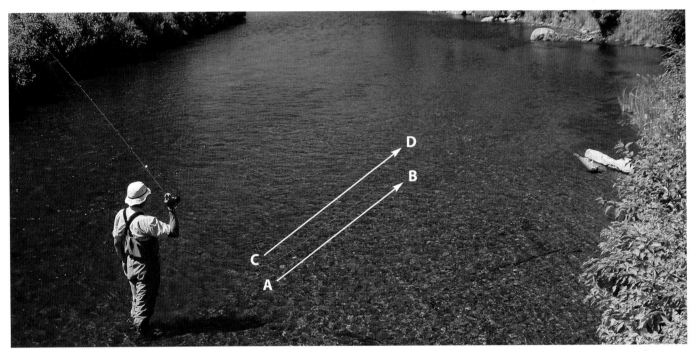

When you are about to make the forward stroke of a roll cast, you want to imagine two rail tracks lying on the water in front of you and extending into the distance. In this example, the line lying on the water (AB) is the right rail track, and the forward cast should be aimed along an imaginary rail track that is close and parallel to the right side track (CD).

The end result of following the rail track principle is a good forward cast that has energy and is efficient.

Due to the load from the D loop and the drag from the line lying on the water, the closer to this rail track principle you follow, the better the cast is. If you make a forward cast at a diverging angle to the rail track, the resultant energy loss would allow for only a very short and inefficient cast.

Imagine if a train hit a set of rail tracks that suddenly diverged. The result would be a catastrophic crash! The same applies with a roll cast. Here the forward cast is directed along the line AB and not parallel to the right rail track CD.

As a result, the forward cast runs out of energy and lands in a heap.

Never make the mistake of aiming your forward cast across the line lying on the water. Unless you do something sneaky, you will find the fly will hook into the line or leader (or you!) as the forward cast tries to unroll.

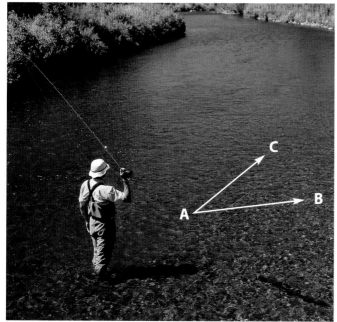

Always listen to your mum! Any kid growing up around a railway is constantly told never to cross the railway line. In this situation, if you were to aim your forward cast over the fly line that is lying on the water (AB) instead of parallel to the right rail track (AC), you would end up with a nasty mess!

A tangled mess results from aiming the forward stroke over the top and crossing the rail track.

Line Stick

One more principle of the roll cast is the significance of the line that is lying on the water at the start of the cast. This is called the anchor. The anchor holds the line on the water and stops the D loop from flicking the fly behind you. All roll casts (and indeed all continuous motion casts) must have an anchor in order to work.

However, the anchor can also create a problem. The water has a thick surface film that can grip the fly line as the forward cast starts. It takes some energy to break this surface tension, and if you have already made your cast, the energy is going to come from the energy that is being used to make the forward cast go out. In other words, you lose energy and end up with a soft cast, or you are unable to make long roll casts.

The secret is to have an anchor, but only a little bit of anchor. Too much is called line stick because that is exactly what happens—the line sticks in the surface. As you get better at the roll cast, you can adjust the amount of line stick by adjusting the angle or height of the rod at the back stop. You can also change the amount of line stuck in the water by changing the timing between making the backcast (such as it is) and the forward cast.

I want to introduce you to something I call point P. Point P is the very spot where the line hanging from the rod in a D loop touches the water.

At all times you want to make sure point P is in front of you when you start the forward cast. If, for whatever reason, point P drifts behind you as you start the forward cast, you will have too much line stick and lose energy. When you are learning a cast, you cannot look at everything at once, and it is often very hard for the beginner to see where point P is. Fortunately, when point P falls behind you, a dead giveaway is a lot of spray as the line rips out of the surface film during the forward cast. You can also hear it—a shripping noise, kind of like a kid drinking soup. The cast should be dead silent as you make the forward cast. Anytime you hear that sound you know you have too much stick.

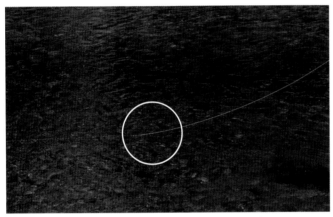

With the rod in the key position, the line hanging down in a D loop will touch the water somewhere. The very point of touch is called point P.

With point P behind you as the forward cast starts, the excess line lying on the water will create a spray as it is torn from the water surface and sound like a kid drinking soup. This cast would fail.

With point P in front of you, there will be no spray or ripping sound as there is no line on the water behind you to rip out; the cast's efficiency is magnified, and it should work perfectly.

In some instances you can drag your backcast behind you with a high rod tip and start your forward cast earlier than normal. Point P will be a bit farther in front of you, which really does help to keep the line stick down to a minimum. However, this will always give a small D loop, so you do not gain much. Nevertheless, as an instructor I encourage you to play around with the position of point P and your D loop size and see what works best for you.

Earlier in this chapter I mentioned a way to increase the D loop size is to tilt the rod farther behind you. This can push the D loop farther back and help load the rod, but it can also push point P behind you and sometimes that isn't worth it. It's all about touch and practice.

In fact, one thing to completely avoid at the end of the back-stroke of a roll cast (or indeed any cast in the spey cast family), is the rod tip dropping toward the water. This will always lay point P behind you and create too much line stick. For those casters that use too much wrist when casting, remember this—a cocked wrist definitely drops the rod tip.

So, in summary, remember you need a D loop to load the rod for the roll cast; you need to keep point P in front of you as you start the forward cast; and you must follow your rail tracks with a good forward cast.

With a cocked or broken wrist, the rod tip will drop behind you. This is not good.

A rod so far behind you, and almost parallel to the water, cannot help but drop lots of line behind you and put point P a long way back. All that will result from this cast is a lot of line spray and noise and a very ineffective forward cast.

Fault Finding

Now to go over a few of the most common mistakes I see when teaching. Nothing beats an actual lesson from a knowledgeable instructor for problem solving, but when you are on your own, practicing and trying to master a new set of casts, it can be useful to know the more common mistakes.

1 **Tangling the line on the forward cast.** This is that dumb move where you have almost invariably crossed over the rail track with your forward cast. It's easy to avoid if you look where your rail track is pointing before you make the cast.

If you make the forward stroke of a roll cast and aim it over the fly line lying on the water in front of you, you will get a tangle in the line. Don't be dumb!

2 **No power in the forward cast; the line falls in a wiggly pile.** There are a few reasons for this. You could be hitting from the top (see the fault-finding section of the next chapter for an explanation of this), or you might just have a lame forward cast, but the most common cause is not driving the forward cast close and parallel to the rail track on the water.

If you aim your forward cast at an angle (such as AB) that is not close and parallel to your rail track (AC), you will have no power and the line will fall in a heap in front of you.

3 **The line wraps around the rod as you form the D loop.** It is very important to make a conscious effort to drag the backcast out to the side of you. If you lift the rod vertically as you come back on the D loop stroke, the line will wrap itself around the rod.

Wrapping the line around the rod when making the D-loop stroke is pretty common and quite frustrating. Usually it comes from a lifting, vertical drag of the rod on the D-loop stroke, not a horizontal, reaching drag to form the D loop.

The roll cast is never going to be a long distance cast, nor will a roll cast ever have the tightest of loops on the forward cast. It can't! Not with the small amount of load the rod gets from the D loop. Without load being derived from the fly line, it has to come from somewhere else— your effort. Simply put, the more effort you put into a cast, the wider your loop will be. For the tightest of loops, you need to use the very least amount of effort, and that is something I shall examine and explain in the next few chapters.

CHAPTER 6

Getting It Out

The roll cast has a problem. It isn't a bad way to make a cast if you have obstructions behind you and don't need to change direction, or get much distance, but you have to have fly line outside the rod tip and in front of you to start the cast. The roll cast is not a good cast if you are fishing a lake or in the salt or fishing a line upstream in a river. In each of these situations, you strip the fly line in as you are fishing. A roll cast is not a good cast for getting that stripped line back out to the fish again—better to use the overhead cast for that.

Of course there are times when you cannot use an overhead cast, so how do you get your line out with the roll cast?

There are at least three ways that I know, use, and teach to get the line out when using the roll cast (or indeed any of the continuous motion casts).

Shooting Line

The most obvious way to get line out is to shoot some line on the forward cast. This does require some speed in the front loop and certainly means that it has to be relatively tight and unroll above the water (not along the water like a barrel of lard). Even so, a very good roll cast will only shoot four or five feet of line on the best of forward casts—and that is assuming that you have enough line outside the rod to make the roll cast in the first place!

One way of getting fly line out with a roll cast is to shoot some line on the forward cast.

A tight loop with good speed that unrolls above the water is essential for this.

The D-Loop Shoot

An easier way is to shoot line on the D-loop stroke. Stroke is really the wrong word in the context of a roll cast, as you really don't make a casting stroke when making the D loop. Instead, you drag the rod into position.

Simply don't hold any fly line while you slowly drag your rod back low and into the key position. Then grab it tight for the forward cast. If you don't hold the line when you drag your rod back slowly, you will see a good number of feet slide through the rod rings while you are dragging the line back. As long as you hold the line tight for the forward stroke, nothing much can go wrong with this method. You could even combine the first and second line-lengthening methods to get the best of both worlds!

Don't hold any fly line at the start of the D-loop stroke/drag.

When you slowly drag the rod back to the key position, loose line will slip through the guides.

As long as you hold the fly line tight for the forward stroke and keep your hands equal distance apart, everything should work out in your favor.

Wiggling the Rod Tip

Perhaps the method that would be counted as the biggest cheat would be the rod tip wiggle. It is also the only way I know to make a roll cast work when you start with as little as three feet of line outside the rod tip. The other two methods work fine if you have line out already, but how do you start? Or what happens if you are stripping in a fly on the lake and pull it to within a few feet of you? Then you use the rod tip wiggle.

Start by stripping the amount of fly line you think you will need off the reel. Then, keeping the rod tip very low and close to the water, wave the rod in smooth side-to-side movements without holding the fly line. As you wave the rod from side to side, line will slip out the guides and land in a wiggly heap in front of you. The key to this move is smoothness. Any jerks or jabs will flick the fly line out of the water, making a cast of sorts and not getting line out.

When you have wiggled the fly line out to the length you want, simply lift the rod to the key position and make a forward cast.

The best way of getting line out of your rod tip initially is the wiggle. Start by stripping all the line you think you will need off the reel.

Then, without holding any of the loose line, start wiggling your rod in long, slow strokes low and close to the water and on either side of where your fly is sitting.

Continue to do this until all the slack has been wiggled out.

Finish off the cast by kicking back your rod in a D-loop stroke, forming a powerful D loop and finishing with a good forward stroke.

The end result—a fast and efficient way to go from zero to sixty (feet) with a continuous motion cast.

I have used this wiggle a thousand times to great effect. I have fished lakes with no backcasting space, using this wiggle to get the line out of the rod rings and then finishing with my roll cast.

I always use this method of getting the line out when I start a day's fishing and have to use a spey cast as my fishing cast.

I have fished for stripers off Cape Cod, from the shore and with tall banks behind me, and used this wiggle move to get the line out before launching a turbo spey (see page 224) to the frenzied feeding fish that have been out of reach to any other fly caster.

The great thing about this is that it is unbelievably easy to do. Most other cool casts that really work are more complicated than they first appear, but not this. Just keep the rod tip low—you need the line stuck on the water and in the surface film to stop the line lifting into the nearest obstruction—the side-to-side waves smooth, then lift to the key position, and complete with a good forward stroke to get the line straight. Easy as pie!

CHAPTER 7

The Double Roll Cast

Continuous Motion Group

The double roll cast is a simple way to get a little more distance than a regular roll cast can. I say simple, but it does take a little practice and good timing—better timing than a roll cast ever does.

The regular roll cast has a small D loop and a fairly substantial amount of line anchored on the water at the start of the forward cast. It also has what I call a passive D loop—a D loop that only has mass and no momentum to help load the rod. These are the reasons that the roll cast is the least efficient cast of all. It also contributes to the roll cast's widest forward loop of any cast.

To get more distance and tighten up the front loop, the cast needs to be more efficient—remember where efficiency comes from in a continuous motion cast? Big D loop, small amount of

When to use this cast:
Increasing distance with a roll cast.

anchor, and least amount of power applied to the forward stroke. This is achieved with the double roll cast.

It really is no more than two roll casts put together. You make the first roll cast, and then while the forward cast is still in the air, you make a second roll cast. Because the fly line is in the air when you start the D-loop stroke of the second roll cast, it comes back toward you much cleaner and easier. It also will have momentum (something that the regular D loop of a roll cast doesn't have), so you are now loading against an aggressive D loop. This gives you a larger D loop, less line anchored on the water, and less need to hit the forward cast so hard. The end result is more efficiency, more distance, and tighter loops.

The double roll cast starts like an ordinary roll cast, with a D loop hanging by your shoulder.

A regular roll cast forward stroke commences, though at a slightly increased elevation.

Before the forward cast of the first roll cast lands, raise the rod tip and start to draw it to the side as part of the next D-loop stroke.

Continue to draw the rod back sideways and then finish with a rise to the key position. This creates a D loop that is larger and has more load than the first roll cast.

The second roll cast forward stroke starts as the D loop touches the water. The forward cast must be precisely timed to reap the rewards of this cast.

But the rewards are more efficiency, higher line speed, and a tighter front loop than the regular roll cast can ever get.

I also use the double roll cast for getting extra line out. As I mentioned in the previous chapter, the regular roll cast is a notoriously poor cast for shooting line, as you can really only shoot a couple of feet during the inefficient forward cast. You can use the ways I outlined in the previous chapter to get out your line, but as far as actually shooting it on the forward cast, the roll cast is pretty poor. Another way to overcome this is to use the double roll cast—shooting a little line on the start of the first roll cast and considerably more line on the forward cast of the second roll cast.

Remember, this isn't a simple cast to get right, but if you can make a reasonable roll cast and can progress to the double roll cast, it is a good step toward the really efficient continuous motion casts.

CHAPTER 8

The Switch Cast

Continuous Motion Group
Airborne Anchor Subgroup

The roll cast forms the foundation of the family of casts known as the spey casts. You have to understand the roll cast before you can move on to something a little more dynamic and useful. You should have a solid foundation of the basics before moving on to more advanced and wonderful casts, so practice the things mentioned in the previous chapters before stepping out, book in hand, turned to this page.

The switch cast is far more dynamic and efficient than the roll cast and the double roll cast and will give you more efficient casts, much greater distance, and start to give you some of those wonderful tight loops that modern casters strive for. It is also an unbelievably satisfying cast to perform.

I'll start by comparing the roll cast we've already looked at with this newer and more dynamic switch cast. When making the D-loop stroke of a roll cast, you slowly drag the fly line back

> **When to use this cast:** no change of direction, obstructions behind, mid- to long distance.

with the rod. You need to ensure that most of the fly line stays on the water in front of you (making it a waterborne anchor cast) and stays under tension throughout the backcast. This gives you a small, passive D loop. A passive D loop hangs from the rod tip behind you, giving only weight to load the rod (and not much at that). The switch cast, on the other hand, has an aggressive D loop. What you should create with a switch cast is a D loop that has weight and momentum. You literally throw the D loop behind you. When you make a forward cast against such a load, the result is awesome. The rod loads deeply, you use a fraction of the effort on the forward cast, and the cast zings out with great speed and energy.

You can condense this into another form of the energy ratio. Simply put, the bigger your load (D loop), the less effort you employ.

A roll cast will load the rod only with a small amount of the potential. The small, passive D loop is motionless and has little mass to flex the rod against. With so little load, the energy ratio is not in your favor, and the forward cast requires a decent amount of power to get anywhere.

With the D loop thrown behind, the increased mass helps load the rod deeply. Not only this, but if you start a forward cast while the D loop has some rear traveling momentum, you will get increased flex against the moving line. This aggressive D loop results in an energy ratio truly in your favor.

Let's take a look at how you make a switch cast.

The switch cast starts with the rod tip low and the line tight and straight in front of you. Unlike the roll cast, you cannot make this cast work if you start with a pile of slack line in front of you. The rod tip on the D-loop stroke actually follows a similar path as the roll cast; however, before the stroke commences, you lift the rod from the water surface to an angle about 30 degrees above the horizontal to unstick some of the line lying on the water. The rod then smoothly transitions into a sweep to the side, passing you and up to the key position. The rod must not dip during this sweep but travel on a pretty flat path with only the slightest of inclines.

The rod is low and the line straight at the start of the switch cast.

Then lift the rod up to about 30 degrees above the water (or 10 o'clock on the clock face) and sweep it to the side in a flat, horizontal move. The lift unsticks the fly line from the water to make the D-loop stroke easy. Note how little fly line is in the water at this stage of the cast.

As the rod sweeps backwards and to the side during the D-loop stroke, it reaches a point level with you (while still traveling flat) where it should accelerate smoothly up to the key position.

Raise the rod to the key position and be ready for the forward cast before any of the fly line has touched the water. The amount of acceleration during the sweep and lift to the key position influences where the anchor is going to land.

If done correctly, the line tip (the anchor) lands level with you and within a rod length to the side of you. The anchor, lying on the water, is straight and taut. At the very moment any part of the fly line or leader touches the water, the forward stroke should start.

The whole D-loop stroke should be one smooth movement; do not pause until the rod is in the key position, and do not jerk or twitch. As the rod passes you and starts to rise to the key position, it should accelerate through this rise slightly and then stop. This acceleration is what makes the cast a switch cast, not a roll cast, and gives you an aggressive D loop, not a passive one. What you are trying to do with this acceleration is get the fly line, leader, and fly out of the water and speeding back toward you—an airborne anchor cast. It is vital your rod gets to the key position and is ready for the forward cast before any fly line (or leader) has touched the water. The line should not be going over your head. If that happens, you are putting far too much acceleration into the cast as well as lifting the rod too steeply. Instead, the line should travel back through the air low and close to the water.

At some stage, gravity will overcome the line's momentum and pull it down onto the water. The faster you accelerate, the farther back the line will travel before gravity takes its toll. Where the line hits the water is a huge part of this cast, and you should really watch where the line does touch the water (the an-chor). If you make a poor acceleration, the anchor will be a long way in front of you and result in a small D loop. With too much power, all the line will fly behind you and into the bushes behind. What you are trying to do is land the anchor level with you and within a rod length to the side of where you are standing. This will give the optimum size of D loop that is aggressive and result in the most efficient energy transfer.

The perfect anchor lands with a straight fly line on the water. If it is straight, it is very easy and efficient to pick out of the water on the forward cast. However, a perfectly straight anchor does not come easily. The subtlest of dips of the rod during the D-loop stroke, or the slightest change in smooth acceleration, will result in an anchor that falls with coils of slack in the line, and the efficiency is gone.

Once you have the D-loop stroke mastered, or at least under control, and can position a straight anchor in the right area, there is the simple matter of the forward cast. I am not going to describe the forward cast again here, or in any other cast further on through this book, as it is its own entity and is covered in an earlier chapter. You can see the end result of the cast here.

The forward stroke should be driven out parallel to the rail track (the anchor) lying on the water. A short positive stop of the rod tip will result in a tight loop.

Keep the rod tip high and still while the loop unrolls. Dropping the rod too early will open up the loop and give you a slack presentation.

The amount of acceleration of the rod during the D-loop stroke changes according to many factors: line length, size and weight of fly, water speed, rod length, depth wading (or height standing on a platform), wind direction, rod action, and line profile, to name but a few. Only practice will give you the feel needed to be able to judge the amount of power required for each cast. In my years of teaching, I have found that the quickest way to get this feel is to always, always, always practice with the same line length, the same rod, the same fly, the same wading depth, and so on. It is impossible for a novice switch caster to get the feel of the cast if there are such variables.

If the rod accelerates too much or the rod comes back on an incline, instead of horizontal, the anchor will fly past you and land somewhere behind—not good if there are obstacles there!

If there is no, or too little, acceleration, the anchor will be a long way in front of you and make a small, inefficient D loop.

If the rod makes a slight dip or downward movement during the D-loop stroke, it will direct line toward the water and ensure the line lands with coils of slack. This is called a piled, or crumpled, anchor. When the forward cast is driven forward against this, it will have little chance of success, pulling out the slack coils instead of efficiently lifting the line out of the water.

Between the D-loop stroke and the forward cast there is a little problem called timing. Back in the chapter on the roll cast, I talked about line stick and point P and the importance of having only a little line on the water at the start of the forward cast. Remember, too much line on the water sucks all the energy from the cast and prevents the line from cleanly breaking away. With the switch cast and all the airborne anchor casts (also called splash and go casts—you'll see why!) timing is the crux of everything. To get the best result when switch casting, watch the tip of the line as it comes back through the air, and as soon as it splashes, start the forward cast. If you wait fractionally too long, too much line will land, and you will never get it out again. If you anticipate the anchor landing and go forward before the line tip touches the water, you will have no grip for the D loop to bite against, and the line will just collapse by your side.

In my classes and demonstrations, I use the analogy of a batsman or hitter (in cricket or baseball) closing their eyes when the ball is thrown at them. It would be pure luck for them to time the swing and hit the ball sweetly. The same with this cast—if you do not watch your line tip as it comes back during the D-loop stroke, you will not see it touch the water and be ready to make the forward cast. You must have your rod upright, at 1 o'clock and in the key position, before your line tip lands.

When learning, and without watching your line tip splash, you are only going to get a good cast by luck. Always watch your line tip!

The perfect switch cast requires perfect timing. Make sure you are ready in the key position and watching the tip of the fly line as it comes back so you can time the forward cast to start as the line tip touches.

If you wait fractionally too long and start the forward cast after the line tip has touched, gravity will pull too much line down onto the water and ensure that point P is behind you. This cast would never get out of the water.

If you anticipate the forward cast and go before any line has touched the water, you will have nothing left to grip the D loop and give it tension. The end result is a very poor cast. All casts in this family have to have some line lying on the water when the forward stroke begins.

I want to reiterate one thing on this cast and that is the rail tracks. If you have formed a good D loop and timed your forward cast perfectly, you can still make a lousy cast by not driving your forward cast parallel to your anchor. It would be a shame to destroy a good cast this way.

Even with a good D loop and perfect timing, you can still make a bad cast. Make sure you drive your forward cast close to, and parallel to, those rail tracks.

Here you see the line tip anchored on the water and pointing in a certain direction; you can also see where I am aiming the forward stroke. The resulting divergence between the two rail tracks will guarantee that the forward cast will collapse.

Fault Finding

Like any other cast, things can go wrong. Here's a short list of the most common faults and how to recognize them.

1 **Too much line stick or anchor.** Recognized by a lot of spray as the line tries to tear itself out of the water on the forward cast. Usually this is either caused by poor timing—starting the forward cast too late—or by dropping the rod tip behind you at the end of the D-loop stroke (usually by cocking the wrist too much).

If there is too much line on the water at the start of the forward cast, the excessive drag will take out all the energy of the forward cast. One cause of this is waiting too long between the end of the D-loop stroke and the start of the forward stroke.

The other cause of too much line stick is dropping the rod tip behind you—usually by breaking the wrist.

2 **A crumpled/piled anchor.** Each anchor, lying on the water, should be straight and taut. If the anchor lies in piles of slack on the water, there will be no tension to load the rod. Dipping the rod on the backcast, instead of having a flat, or slightly rising D-loop stroke, causes the piled anchor.

A piled anchor lands with slack waves and wiggles and should be avoided. Usually a dip in the rod tip on the D-loop stroke causes this. A perfect anchor should be dead straight and taut and is formed by a flat rod path on the D-loop stroke.

3 **No speed in the line on the forward stroke, which dribbles into the water in front.** This is caused by a bad case of the creeps! Or to put it in casting terms, creeping. Many casters find it difficult to hold the rod motionless in the key position until the anchor point touches. If you slightly anticipate the forward cast and creep, or drift the rod, forward, and then make the forward cast, you will find that the rod has no forward stroke left. The result is a rod with no load and a forward loop that fails miserably.

Creep causes the front loop to be angled down toward the water at a descending trajectory and have no speed or power. It is a result of the rod creeping forward while you are waiting for the anchor to land. From this crept position, the rod has no stroke length and therefore cannot generate power into the line. The rod will also have passed the vertical and so the forward stroke is downwards, hence the low trajectory loop.

4 **The forward loop climbs steeply in the air and has no power.** Another forward stroke problem is hitting from the top. In the eagerness to make a forward stroke, many casters jump into the forward cast with speed. They forget the ABCs I talked about in the chapter on the forward stroke. If the rod starts the forward cast with a sudden burst of power, instead of with a smooth acceleration, it will fire the forward loop in a climbing trajectory, usually resulting in a tailing loop, and have no power.

A forward cast that climbs steeply, with no power and that usually snags itself, is caused by too sudden a burst of power at the start of the forward stroke. The correct forward stroke has a smooth acceleration.

5 **The front loop of the forward cast tangles on itself (a tailing loop).** A tailing loop isn't such a common problem with the continuous motion casts as it is with the to-and-fro casts. However, it happens. There are many causes of a tailing loop, but the the most common one with these casts is an uneven acceleration throughout the forward stroke. Keep the rod acceleration smooth.

A forward cast that has a sharp snap of power in the middle of the casting stroke instead of a smooth acceleration will result in a tailing loop. This creates a tangle or wind knot in the line or leader.

The creeping problem, hitting from the top, and the tailing loop are common to all casts—back and forth, continuous motion, or others. Look out for them and develop a solid forward stroke that has none of these problems. I am not going to mention these problems again with any of the other casts, but remember to watch the speed and angle of incline of your front loop with all casts and refer back here if such problematic loops start to appear.

CHAPTER 9

The Single Spey

Continuous Motion Group
Airborne Anchor Subgroup

The single spey is the first of the true spey casts. It seems to have been pigeonholed as a cast for the long rods: two-handed rods, double-handed rods, salmon rods, spey rods, whatever you like to call them. This is especially true in the United States, where spey casting is relatively new. However, nothing could be further from the truth. You can't tell me that obstacles behind a fly fisher are the sole prerogative of someone fishing for salmon or steelhead! True, the cast was invented in Scotland on the River Spey in the mid 1800s, and it was used for salmon and involved big rods, but the essence of the spey casts is that they are highly efficient change-of-direction casts—particularly useful when an obstacle prevents you from making a regular overhead cast. It doesn't matter if you are fishing for steelhead, salmon, trout, carp, or even bonefish, if you want to change direction quickly, or if you have something behind you, the spey casts will see you right!

Most of my spey casting was learned and used in Devon, England—on rivers such as the Taw, Torridge, and Bray. The Bray, in particular, was my favorite, but being only about twenty-five feet wide and full of wild brown trout between 6 and 12 inches, it was not a river for the long salmon rod. My standard outfit on this river was a 6-foot, 6-inch rod with a

> **When to use this cast:** changes of direction, obstructions behind, wind blowing upstream.
> **Hand to use:** Right hand for a direction change to the right, left hand (or backhand) for a direction change to the left.

double-taper #2 line. The river is overhung with trees and bushes and is deceptively deep, with some pools, like Black Pool, as much as fifteen-feet deep. To fish this river at all, you have to wade along the shallower margins and use spey casts just to get your fly to a fish. Of course you could go to the open pools where you could fish from the bank with an overhead cast, but so could everyone else—and there were not so many fish in these stretches!

So, the spey casts (as a group) have a very important role for the single-handed rod fly fisher, and the single spey is where we are going to start.

Like all the change-of-direction casts, I am going to describe this cast as if you are fishing a river, swinging a fly across the current and letting it come to rest on the dangle (directly downstream of you). The cast is used to change direction and put the fly and line back across the current at an angle of between 45 and 60 degrees. However, don't think that it is only for these situations. These are the easiest situations for me to describe the cast, but indeed, once you can make a single spey cast, you will use it for fishing dry flies upstream, for targeting fast-traveling bonefish on a flat, or for cruising trout in a lake or any place, in fact, that requires a change-of-direction cast.

Understanding the Single Spey

Remember the rail track analogy? Let's go back to that for a moment. The single spey changes direction; the roll cast and switch cast do not. If you want to make a change-of-direction cast, all you do is reposition your rail track—line it up with where you want your fly to go—and then finish with a good D loop and forward stroke.

The single spey is just one way of repositioning the fly line to get the right rail tracks. It is probably one of the hardest spey casts to learn in its truest form, but generally will give the competent caster the most distance, as well as the most efficiency.

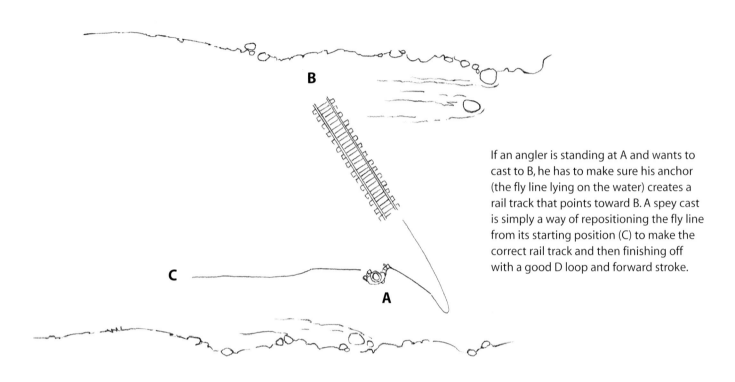

If an angler is standing at A and wants to cast to B, he has to make sure his anchor (the fly line lying on the water) creates a rail track that points toward B. A spey cast is simply a way of repositioning the fly line from its starting position (C) to make the correct rail track and then finishing off with a good D loop and forward stroke.

Crude Spey, Stage 1

The easiest way to learn the single spey is to break it down to the barest of bones. My dad used to say, "Learn it the army way"—by numbers! You can learn this cast (after a quick demonstration) by following three simple words: flop, drag, and chop. I call it the crude spey because it is no more than a starting point on the road to learning the more efficient modern spey, but it works, and I guarantee there is no better way to understand what you are trying to do, and what rod moves there are, for learning the true single spey.

Let's look at it in a step-by-step sequence. Assume you are on the left bank of a river (the current flowing from right to left), the line has washed tight, downstream of you, and you need to cast your line across the river. First you must move the rail track from downstream to across-stream.

You do this by slowly bringing your rod in toward the near bank and pointing over your left shoulder. You then sweep your rod up and over you and across the river, aiming for a point directly opposite you. If your line is tight when you start and you have enough lift and oomph in the stroke, you will flop the line across the river. It will land in a wiggly heap, but at least it is in the right sort of place.

The first move of the simplest version of the spey cast starts with your fly line washed downstream of you. Swing the rod slowly in toward the near bank, but keep the hand and rod on the downstream side of your body.

With a lifting move, sweep the rod over your head.

Continue sweeping the rod across the river, aiming at a point directly opposite you, and finish with the rod tip low and close to the water.

If you do this correctly, you will lay the fly line in a wiggly heap on the water in front of you.

Crude Spey, Stage 2

Once your line is across the river, you have finished the hardest part of this cast. You have also ensured your safety for the next stage, which requires a D loop. As I talked about in the roll cast chapter, you simply drag the rod low and sideways on your upstream side, lifting the rod to the key position as it gets level with you. Make sure your fly, leader, and fly line stay on the water throughout the drag, and make sure you form a small, passive D loop behind you. You will probably need to turn your body a little, as one of the key factors to the success of the change-of-direction casts is getting your rod directly opposite where you want to land your fly. This usually involves a rotation of the body, from ankles, knees, hips, and shoulders.

The second stage of this cast is a drag! Keeping your fly, leader, and line on the water, slowly drag your rod to your upstream side, making sure it stays low and flat through the drag.

Keep dragging the rod around to your upstream side.

As you do that, lift to the key position. Your rod should be turned so that it is opposite where you are going to aim your forward cast, and you should have a D loop hanging from the rod, also opposite your target. You should have a perfect rail track at this stage (see arrow) to aim at.

Crude Spey, Stage 3

Once your rod is in the key position opposite your target and once a D loop has formed opposite your target, you finish this cast off with a forward stroke. Remember to aim your forward cast close and parallel to the line lying on the water, and for goodness sake don't muck it up by crossing over the line (rail track)!

The final stage of the crude spey is the forward stroke. From the key position, just finish the cast off with the forward stroke of the roll cast. Do not cross over the line lying on the water, and aim close and parallel to the rail track.

Watch the loop unroll in the air.

The loop lands softly and cleanly on the water.

This cast is so easy to learn. If you see it and follow the simple explanation on the previous pages, you can learn it in less than a minute, provided you can make a good roll cast and understand the rail track principle completely.

You should not have a physical aiming point when you start the cast. Don't say, "I am going to aim at that tree," and go through stage 1 and stage 2 and then aim stage 3 at that tree. Learn the value of the rail tracks, and wherever your line is lying on the water at the end of the D-loop stroke, make the correct forward cast, close and parallel to that line. Only if your line is on the water facing that tree when you are in the key position should you aim at the tree. This isn't going to happen every time when you are learning.

I can't stress this enough for the beginner. Get used to finding your rail track when you are in the key position and making a good cast, regardless of where you had planned on casting.

Practice this, and it will quickly become natural. Once it is natural, you will find that it doesn't take any time at all to get the hang of positioning the rail track so that it is lined up for your actual target. Then you are ready for the next step in your evolution as a spey caster.

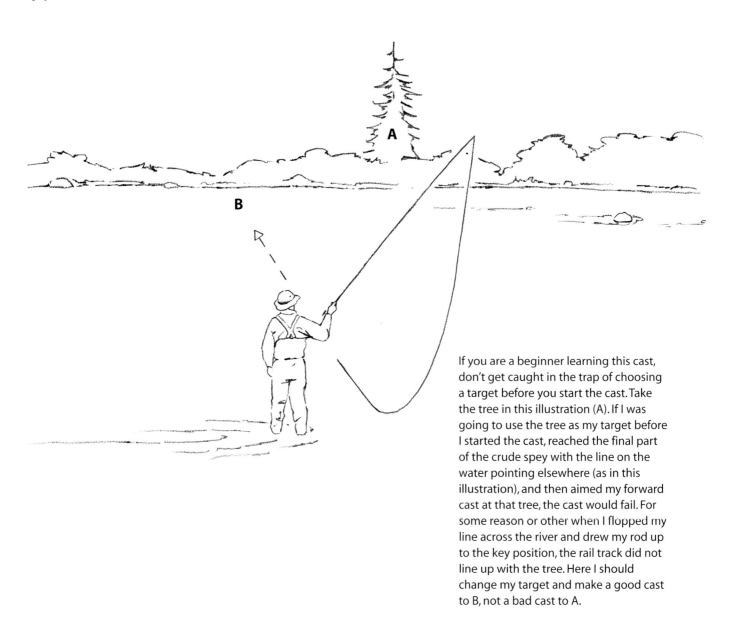

If you are a beginner learning this cast, don't get caught in the trap of choosing a target before you start the cast. Take the tree in this illustration (A). If I was going to use the tree as my target before I started the cast, reached the final part of the crude spey with the line on the water pointing elsewhere (as in this illustration), and then aimed my forward cast at that tree, the cast would fail. For some reason or other when I flopped my line across the river and drew my rod up to the key position, the rail track did not line up with the tree. Here I should change my target and make a good cast to B, not a bad cast to A.

The Traditional Single Spey

The next step is to eliminate one of the moves and make this cast more efficient and more a thing of beauty. This is achieved with the traditional single spey. The fastest way to master the single spey cast is to start with the crude spey, which gives you a feel for what you are trying to do and ingrains a good muscle memory of your rod and arm movements. But it is segmented and jerky—crude, if you like. The traditional single spey is much more graceful, a thing of beauty to watch, ballet with a fly line.

To make a traditional spey, you simply merge stage 1 and stage 2 of the crude spey. In other words, you start with your rod to your inside and downstream shoulder, and then sweep the rod over and across the river and drag the rod back and up to 1 o'clock and the key position before any fly line lands. The first stage and second stage become one and look like this:

1

2

3

4

5

6

7

8

9

At this stage, the D-loop stroke is finished and the entire fly line is airborne. You must wait until the fly line first touches the water before finishing off the cast with the forward stroke. The rest of it is as follows:

10

11

12

13

14

When you are forming the D loop with the crude spey, you will find that the fly line lands on the water before you have reached the key position. However, with the traditional single spey, you must be in the key position before the fly line lands. This is what keeps the energy in the cast and makes it far more dynamic and efficient.

At this point of the crude spey, you would stop the rod and let the line land on the water before dragging back a D loop for stage 2. However, as you can see, the line is still in midair here and the rod flexed, starting to come back on the D-loop stroke.

In this photo you can see that the rod is in the key position and the line still not on the water. Because the traditional spey has an airborne anchor, the rod must get into the key position before any fly line touches the water. You must then wait until the line tip (or the leader) lands and then promptly start the forward cast.

The outbound cast has a nice tight loop and is far more efficient than in the crude spey. This is because the merging of stages 1 and 2 gives a much more aggressive D loop and loses less line speed and energy due to it being stuck on the water. You can use less effort and get a tighter, more efficient loop.

Tempting as it may be for the reader to start with this cast, I'd strongly advise throwing a few crude speys first. A little work on the basics pays dividends in the long run with form, understanding, and muscle memory. I am sure you want to be an effortless caster, throwing razor-tight loops and impressing all the anglers watching, but that will come. Master your foundation first!

Efficient casts, whether continuous motion or the to-and-fro casts, stem from a good load on the backcast. If your rod is loaded, you don't need to work so hard. Remember the energy ratio.

As you get better at the traditional spey, start to play with it. The faster you throw your D loop back, the larger it will be. Initially, when most casters move from the crude spey to the traditional spey, they merge the two stages (one and two) together, keeping the rod traveling at one speed. As you get better and can control your move (rather than react in panic), start to accelerate as the rod comes back on the D-loop stroke, and see what this will do for you. The D loop will be bigger, and the cast more efficient.

The first few traditional speys you throw will have one speed of rod movement from the start of the cast to the completion of the D-loop stroke. This will produce a nice traditional single spey, but with a relatively small D loop.

With practice, and a little awareness of your arm and hand movements, you can start to accelerate on the D-loop stroke. This will give you a larger D loop, more load, and will mean you can use less effort on the forward cast. Look how much bigger the D loop is here compared with the previous photo.

This acceleration should only be directly opposite your target. If you accelerate too early, you will throw your D loop too far upstream and have no direct load on the rod as the forward cast starts. Too late an acceleration will throw the D loop too far behind you and again ensure a poor load for the forward cast. In a perfect cast, your D loop is exactly opposite your forward cast.

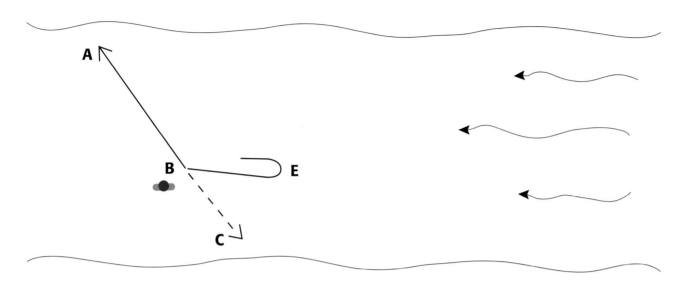

In this illustration, I have marked a few reference lines. AB is my intended target line, and BC is directly opposite—where the D loop should end up. If I make the D-loop stroke of the traditional spey and accelerate the formation of the D loop too early, it will throw the D loop too far upstream (BE). With a D loop at BE and a forward cast toward AB, you will find there is no load on the rod and the cast will fall in a miserable heap.

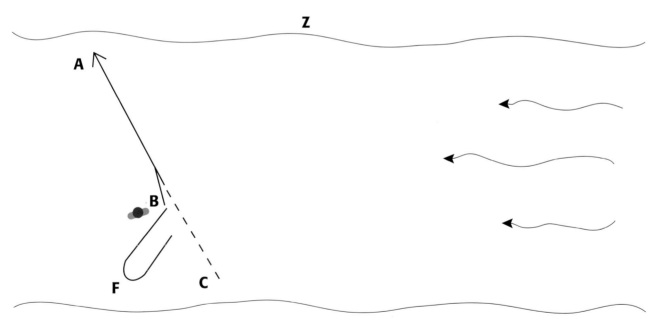

In the same vein, if I delay the acceleration of the D loop to FZ, the D loop will again be misaligned with my intended cast (AB), and the cast will fail. If this makes any sense to you, you should be able to answer this question: where should the forward cast be aimed if the D loop is at FZ?

A poorly aligned D loop is a major fault with casters learning these continuous motion casts. If you answered, "Directly opposite the D loop" or "Along the FZ plane," on that question in the below illustration, you are right. Give yourself a pat on the back!

The Modern Single Spey

Like any casting technique, as you get more comfortable with what you are doing, you should refine your technique. Don't rest on your laurels and be content with what you are doing—strive to develop more advanced techniques. Become a Jedi Spey Master!

The modern single spey takes more precision than the traditional single spey. It requires better technique, a more precise rod path, and a very controlled speed. But when mastered, it is so satisfying, so efficient, and so powerful that it is the only way for a disciple of the spey to go. You probably won't catch any more fish with this cast, not if you can perform the traditional single spey well, but this is not a book on catching fish!

The modern single spey relies on more flat movements of the rod. I believe that if you are casting and make a movement of the rod, it should have a direct and positive effect on the line. To that extent, the only directional movement of the rod that really helps make a cast (load the rod) is horizontal. Moving your rod up and down really does not add much flex to the rod. However, if you have fly line on the water (straight and tight) and move your rod horizontally and directly opposite that fly line, you will see the rod flex much more. It is this principle that forms the foundation of the modern single spey.

The first step of this cast is to start with your rod angled some degrees across the water—more toward your target than downstream or behind you. (Both the crude and traditional single spey start with the rod angled behind you, pointing toward the bank you are casting from.) This means that when you make the D-loop stroke, your rod is traveling in a straight, efficient plane.

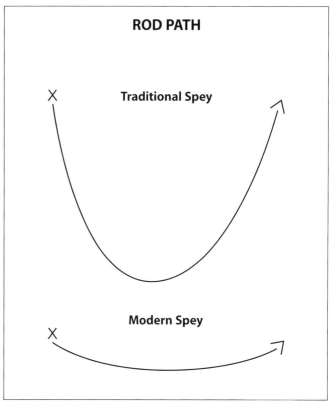

If you were to imagine that the rod had a pencil lashed to the tip and you were to draw the rod path of the D-loop stroke of the traditional spey, you would get a deep U shape. With the modern spey, you would get a very shallow saucer—much more efficient.

The crude and traditional single speys start with the rod angled back toward the bank you are standing by. The modern single spey starts with the rod angled out toward the river.

A D-loop stroke that starts with the rod angled in toward the near bank (as with the crude and traditional speys) creates the initial momentum of the rod out toward the middle of the river (line AB), and then, as the rod comes back to complete the D-loop stroke, the momentum changes and comes behind the caster (BC). Then the forward stroke (CD) finishes off the cast.

By starting with the rod angled out toward the river, you keep a much straighter and more direct rod path on the D-loop stroke (AB). This is more efficient and results in much more load and rod flex.

The other advantage of starting the rod angled across the river is that the rod tip can make the D-loop stroke with only the subtlest of rod tip dips. You can position the anchor by controlling the speed of the rod stroke—not by dipping the rod to aim the anchor point onto the water (as with the crude and traditional versions). This advantage goes back to what I was saying earlier about how a flat, horizontal rod path will load the rod better than a rod path that involves lots of ups and downs.

With the rod angled across the river some 45 degrees, the cast starts with a lift of the rod to unstick some of the line from the water. The lift should be slow and smooth and perfectly vertical. At the top of the lift and without a pause, instantly dip the rod to form a smooth, shallow saucer shape, accelerating as the rod starts to rise from the saucer. You should rotate from the hips and with the shoulders during the saucer shape to ensure that the rod finishes in the key position. Watch the tip of the fly line as it comes back through the air and, as it touches the water and forms the anchor, make the forward cast. Remember, this is an airborne anchor cast, so do not wait for the line tip to settle.

Start with the rod angled about 45 degrees across the river and low.

Slowly and smoothly raise the rod in a vertical plane to a 10 o'clock position. Do not lift the rod at any angle, but keep it dead vertical.

At the top of the lift, and without any pause, sweep the rod round in a shallow saucer shape, accelerating as the rod rises to the key position.

Hold in the key position until the line tip splashes on the water. You should angle the rod at about 1 o'clock behind you and rotate it so it is directly opposite your target.

The instant the first piece of fly line (or leader) hits the water, start the forward stroke.

Drive the forward cast out, parallel to the rail track.

Watch the loop unroll beautifully.

While this style is based on starting with the rod angled across the river, there is a limit to how far across you can point. Regardless of where you want to aim your forward stroke, do not start with your rod more than 45 degrees across the current. If you start with your rod too square, you will have little or no effect in creating a powerful D loop.

There is one very important rule to remember with this modern style: it is great for angle changes up to 60 degrees or so. For a wider angle change (and in particular an angle change more than 90 degrees), the traditional style will serve you better.

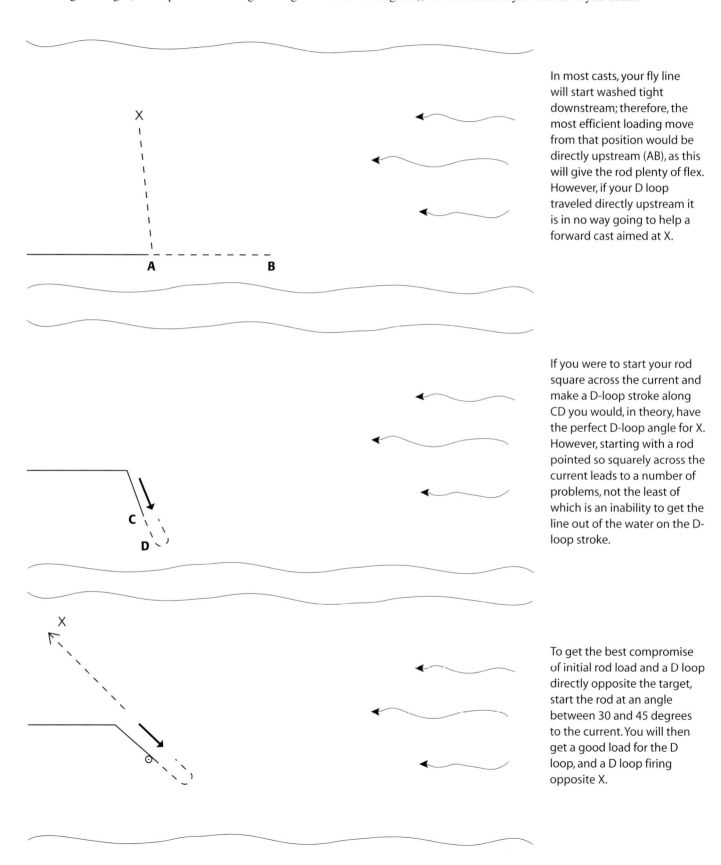

In most casts, your fly line will start washed tight downstream; therefore, the most efficient loading move from that position would be directly upstream (AB), as this will give the rod plenty of flex. However, if your D loop traveled directly upstream it is in no way going to help a forward cast aimed at X.

If you were to start your rod square across the current and make a D-loop stroke along CD you would, in theory, have the perfect D-loop angle for X. However, starting with a rod pointed so squarely across the current leads to a number of problems, not the least of which is an inability to get the line out of the water on the D-loop stroke.

To get the best compromise of initial rod load and a D loop directly opposite the target, start the rod at an angle between 30 and 45 degrees to the current. You will then get a good load for the D loop, and a D loop firing opposite X.

Fault Finding

Let's take a look at the most common faults with this cast.

1 **The line wraps around the rod (or you) while making the D-loop stroke.** This is either caused by having some slack in the line prior to the start of the cast or by angling the rod more than 45 degrees across the river at the start of the D-loop stroke.

This problem is caused by either starting the rod too square or having slack in the line at the start of the D-loop stroke. Line wrapped in front of you like this will only tangle on the forward cast.

2 **The line does not come out of the water when the D-loop stroke is made.** Either the rod did not rise high enough on the initial lift to unstick the fly line, or there was a pause between the vertical lift and the start of the dip, which allowed the line to settle back on the water. It could also be caused be a weak, or lack of, acceleration into the key position.

If the line does not come out of the water when the D-loop stroke is made, it is because either there was a pause at the top of the initial lift (allowing the line to sink back into the water) or the lift was not high enough for that length of line.

3 **Bloody L anchor.** The bloody L anchor is the term for an anchor that does not lie on the water in a straight line, pointing directly toward the target. The L shape of the line has the majority of the rail track pointing toward the target, but the tail that is hooked to the side will take out every ounce of energy in the cast. It will be like the forward cast has hit a brick wall. This is usually caused by not starting the shallow saucer shape immediately at the top of the lift. It can also be caused by making more of a U shape—too deep a dip—than the shallow saucer necessary.

The bloody L anchor is usually caused by the rod traveling laterally at the top of the initial lift and not instantaneously starting the saucer-shaped dip, though it could also be caused by too deep a dip when making the D-loop stroke. Note the L shape of the fly line sitting on the water.

4 **The line does not come out of the water when the forward stroke is made.** There are a number of causes for this—bad timing, not enough D loop to load the rod, or a weak forward cast, but the number one cause is breaking the rail track rule. Invariably, everyone starting off on this cast will not focus on where the line anchors on the water, and they pop off their forward cast in some unknown direction. Every single one of these casts has to follow the rail track in order to be efficient.

A cast will fail every time if the forward stroke does not follow the anchor that is lying on the water. Here the anchor (AB) is a long way upstream. For this cast to work, you would have to note this and aim the forward stroke parallel and close to AB, not to the large rock that was the intended target!

5 The forward loop collides into the line as it unrolls (called a collision loop). It is vital, on this cast, that the anchor point is on the upstream side of the target. If not, you will cross the rail track and tangle. The other option is that the D loop was not directly opposite the target. In this scenario, the caster tries to fire the line in a different direction than where the forward cast is being driven and the opposing forces make the lines collide.

A collision loop usually results when the D loop is not aligned with the forward cast. Here you can see the majority of the forward cast is heading across the river, but the last couple of feet of line is pointing up and down the river. This is a very clear indication that the D loop was too far upriver for the angle cast. Remember, it should be directly opposite where the forward cast aims.

This cast will certainly result in a collision loop—look where the D loop is aiming (AB) and where the forward cast is lined up (CD). No chance of any success here!

So, the longest chapter in this book comes to a close! I make no apologies for writing such a long thesis on this cast. I have taught it enough to know that learning it step by step—crude spey, traditional spey, and finally modern spey—ultimately gives the novice spey caster a more solid foundation and a quicker learning curve. Remember that this has the reputation of being the hardest of the spey casts to learn—justifiably so, I might add!

CHAPTER 10

The Double Spey

Continuous Motion Group
Waterborne Anchor Subgroup

> **When to use this cast:** changes of direction, obstructions behind, wind blowing downstream.
>
> **Hand to use:** Right hand for a direction change to the left, left hand (or backhand) for a direction change to the right.

As a caster it is useful to be able to cast in all sorts of conditions, and the very first lesson to learn with the double spey is that you use this cast when the wind is blowing downstream with the current. If you make a single spey when the wind is in this direction, you will endanger yourself. You make the single spey with your upstream hand; if you are on the left side of the river (the river flowing from right to left), you would make this cast with your right hand. If the wind is blowing downstream in this situation it will be blowing on your right-hand side, so any cast with the right hand is risky. On this side of the river, and with this wind, the safe cast is made from your left side, where the wind will blow your line away from you and the rod and not into it, and that is the double spey.

The ideal situation is to actually change hands and use your left hand for the cast, but many casters are concerned they have no ability with their weaker hand. If that is the case, you can make the cast backhanded—still with your dominant hand, but off the opposite (and correct) shoulder.

This is the simplest and most logical reason to use the double spey cast. Another one could be that you just want to learn more casts—more power to you!

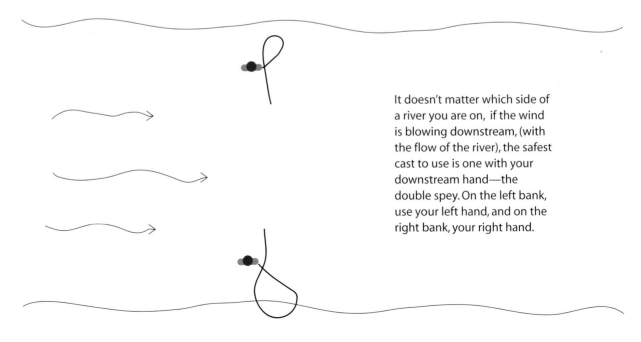

It doesn't matter which side of a river you are on, if the wind is blowing downstream, (with the flow of the river), the safest cast to use is one with your downstream hand—the double spey. On the left bank, use your left hand, and on the right bank, your right hand.

If the river is flowing from left to right, or you want to make this cast to change direction from your right-hand side toward the left, you need to cast with your right hand.

If you are right-handed and the river is flowing from right to left, or the direction change is from your left side toward the right, you should cast with your left hand.

The alternative is to use the right hand and tilt the hand across the body to make a backhanded cast.

I want to describe the cast as though you are standing in a river with the line washed parallel to the bank you are fishing from (on the dangle) and you need to make a directional change cast, with limited backcasting space. As with the single spey, once you have mastered this cast you will find plenty of other uses for the double spey—not just swinging a fly across the river with a downstream blowing wind. But for ease of learning, this scenario is the easiest to understand.

The double spey is a member of the waterborne anchor subgroup, so during the entire D-loop stroke the line should stay on the water. This is an important thing to remember even before you start the cast.

The double spey consists of two moves, or strokes, (hence the word "double") before the forward stroke delivers the fly out to the target: the setup stroke and the D-loop stroke. Let's take a look at the setup stroke.

The Setup Stroke

The setup stroke of the double spey is the first move you make. If you are a right-handed caster, the line will start on the right-hand side of your body, washed tight downstream, with your rod tip also pointing directly downstream. Start the cast with a slow lift of the rod until it is at about the 1:30 position, then stop. The stop is very important. You need to stop the rod until the line you have lifted off the water has settled back down onto the water again and is motionless.

When the line has settled back on the water and point P is close to you, the rod should sweep smoothly over the top of your head and finish pointing directly upstream and close to the water. The object of this move is to lift the fly line, leader, and fly out of the water and reposition them on the water farther upstream. Thus the setup stroke ends.

Start the double spey with the line washed to your right (for a right-handed caster), directly downstream and taut. The rod tip should start low and pointing at the fly line, and your target is directly opposite you.

The beginning of the setup stroke commences raising the rod tip to about 1:30 and then stopping.

The stop should be long enough to allow the lifted line to drop back on the water, for point P (circled) to settle back close to you, and for the line to stop all momentum.

Once the line has settled back in the water and point P has been established, sweep the rod upstream and over your head.

There needs to be enough speed in the sweep to lift all the fly line out of the water. Continue to sweep the rod and angle it down toward the water surface directly on your left-hand side.

The rod finishes low and close to the water, pointing directly upstream. At this stage the entire fly line is still in the air but is starting to drop toward the water surface.

Keep the rod tip in this finished position as the line starts to land on the water. If done correctly, the tip of the fly line should land slightly downstream of you.

The D-Loop Stroke

When the setup stroke has been completed, you are ready for the D-loop stroke. The D-loop stroke is just that—a rod movement designed to produce a D loop. Like all D loops, you should finish this stroke with the D loop directly opposite the target and a suitable and straight rail track running in that general direction

From the low rod position at the end of the setup stroke, sweep the rod back downstream and behind you into the key position. The sweep should be even paced and smooth and, most important, on a slight but steady incline up to the key position—never dip the rod throughout the sweep.

The D-loop stroke starts with sweeping the rod in a low, flat movement back toward your right.

As you sweep the rod toward the right and downstream, it follows a slight incline, rising gradually and smoothly as it sweeps downstream.

The rod sweep will start to tear the fly line out of the water, creating a spray of water.

The rod tip continues its rising, smooth sweep until it is opposite the chosen target.

Here you must wait in the key position until all the fly line has swept round into a D loop behind you and opposite where you intend the forward cast to be aimed.

The Forward Stroke

Once you are at this stage, completing the cast is easy, provided you aim your forward stroke close and parallel to the rail track you have set up. The only thing to note at this stage is that there is a timing issue. When the D-loop stroke is finished and the rod is in the key position, pause before the forward stroke commences. This pause is just long enough for the D loop to stop traveling. Do not go forward while the D loop has momentum—otherwise you will lose your anchor—and do not wait so long that your D loop drops onto the water, with point P behind, and sticks in the surface film.

With a good rail track and no bloody L, all that remains is a nice forward stroke toward the target.

The front loop should be tight and smooth.

On the final presentation of a good double spey, the forward cast unrolls completely in the air before the leader, fly, and fly line land at the same moment.

That is the simple and short way of looking at the very basic movements of this cast, and now would be a good time for you, if you are a novice at this cast, to close this book and work on these simple basics.

However, like all casts there is more to it than the very basics, and I want to elaborate a little more here and make you aware of some of the key factors.

There is a reason the setup stroke is so named—it sets up the success of the cast. What you are trying to do is position the tip of the fly line in a direct line with your target. This will make it easy to have a rail track pointing toward your target after the D-loop stroke and, therefore, a successful forward stroke.

As a beginner, I would strongly advise not actually having a target. The first few times you do this, you will have no control of the position of your line tip. Instead, use the position of the line tip as your target and mentally prepare yourself to make your forward cast over the spot where the line tip is lying.

At the end of the setup stroke, find the position of the line tip and get ready to make your cast in this direction. Regardless of where you want your cast to go, use the line tip as your indicator, and if necessary, change your target to reflect the line tip's position. In this photo the line tip is well downstream of me. If I drew a line from me in the general direction of the line tip (AB), this would be my target—not the line AX that I had intended.

In this situation the line tip has come a long way past my AX target line. No problem. I draw my imaginary line in the direction of the line tip again (AB) and use this direction for a successful forward stroke.

In the ideal setup stroke, the line tip lands in line just downstream of the AX line. Then you can aim the forward stroke where you originally intended.

Practice this setup stroke often, until you get good at placing the line tip where you want. Once you have achieved control of your line tip's landing position, you can start to choose a target to aim at. Many factors will influence the amount of power you need in the sweep to get the line tip to drop in the correct position—size of fly, length of line, depth of fly, length of rod, current speed, and depth of wading, to name just a few. When practicing, always start with your rod in the same 1:30 position. If you alter this, you are adding another variable to your positioning skills, and anyone learning this cast does not need variables!

Back to the D-loop stroke. The rod should sweep and rise in a continuous and smooth incline to the key position—no dip of the rod whatsoever—during the D-loop stroke. A dip is bad; I'll explain why shortly.

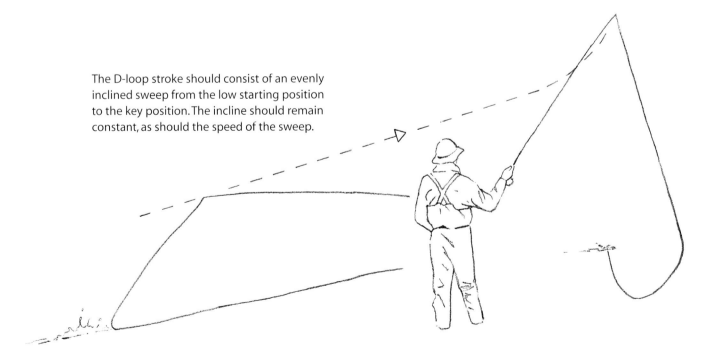

The D-loop stroke should consist of an evenly inclined sweep from the low starting position to the key position. The incline should remain constant, as should the speed of the sweep.

During the D-loop stroke, you are trying to reposition the line from an upstream/downstream position (where it has landed on the setup stroke) to a perfect rail track to your target. For this to happen, you need enough speed in the rod sweep to put the right amount of momentum into the fly line to break the water surface tension and allow it to align with your target.

The right amount of incline and the right amount of sweep speed will make the very tip of the fly line pirouette on the water. All fly line outside of this tip will sweep around this pirouette point and make a nice rail track for the very best forward cast.

If you are really, really good at this and have the perfect touch, the line tip is not the pirouette point, the fly is.

The perfect speed and incline of the D-loop stroke allows the entire fly line to reposition itself from an upstream/downstream position to a rail track aimed directly at your target.

If the sweep is too slow, or the incline too shallow (or the rod tip dips during the D-loop stroke), there will only be enough momentum to move part of the line lying on the water, and the end result is a bloody L (because of the L shape of the line lying on the water). The bigger the tail of the L, the worse the forward cast will be.

Too fast a sweep, or too steep an incline, will lift all the fly line out of the water.

The fly line will land neatly into the nearest bush behind you.

The most perfect D-loop stroke has the right angle and speed to leave the fly on the water, but make it pirouette on the water and align even its tail feathers with the target. This is perfection, but don't worry if you can't get this right. You will still get an excellent result if you can get the line tip to pirouette.

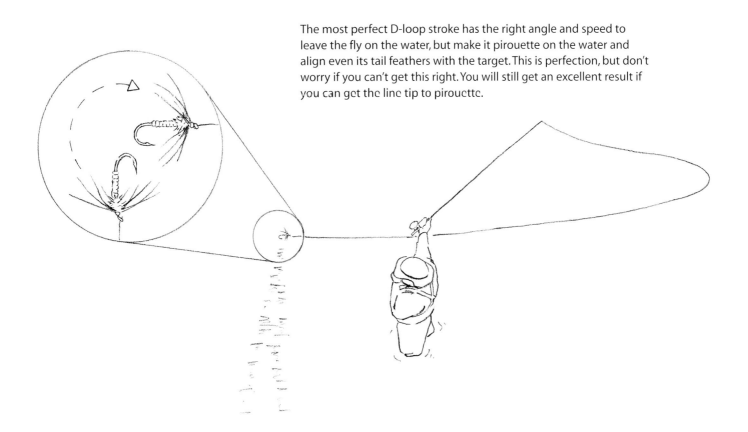

Getting more technical

As in any of the continuous motion casts, the successful caster should have the ability to control how big his D loop is. In an earlier chapter I explained how the largest D loop gives the most load to the rod and therefore requires the least amount of effort to make the cast go out. A large D loop will also give the tightest of front loops, as well as the most distance. Okay, so what happens when you arrive at a small creek and need to stay close to the bank? Any size of D loop will snag the obstacles behind. In situations like this, you need to create a small D loop. I don't want anyone to say, "Hey, that book by the Englishman was useless; all I ever do is snag stuff behind me!" To save such unworthy comments, let me give you a couple of tips.

1 **The D-loop size is controlled by how fast the D-loop stroke is.** Sounds obvious, right? Many people forget that and have a set D-loop stroke regardless of what is behind. It's like mending: I see so many people who get into the habit of mending the line when fishing that they do it at all times—when it is needed, when it is not needed, and when it is positively a "no". With a double spey (or with any continuous motion cast, actually), when you have room behind you, make sure you have a nice fast D-loop stroke and throw back that large load, giving yourself a good sized D loop that will contribute to a nice, efficient cast. When you are tight to obstructions, have a slow D-loop stroke and let the D loop hang lifeless by your shoulder. Don't automatically have one D-loop stroke speed!

When you have room behind you, a large D loop will help with an effortless and beautiful cast.

When room behind is restricted, a small D loop is required. This will result in less distance and, most important, you need more of a "whack" on the forward cast to get the rod to load. However, it does prevent getting your D loop caught in the bushes behind!

2 **The other tip on D-loop size requires going back to the position of the line tip at the end of the setup stroke.** If you sweep your rod almost vertically over your head on the setup stroke, you will land the fly line close to your feet. This has the potential to create a large D loop. Assuming you get the pirouette right, virtually all the line you have outside your rod tip will turn into a D loop. If, on the other hand, you sweep the rod tip in less of a vertical plane and reach out on the setup stroke, you will land the line a long way in front of you. With the right pirouette, you will have a much smaller D loop.

You will only have success with this smaller D loop with a shorter line length and more power on the forward cast. Don't expect an efficient, long cast with no load to help, but at least you should be able to fish areas with only a couple of feet of room behind.

To make the largest of D loops, start the setup stroke in the usual position.

Sweep the rod tip in a vertical plane over the top of your head.

The vertical sweep will ensure the line lands close to you. With a good pirouette, almost all the fly line will turn into a large D loop.

In tight situations and when you want a smaller D loop, start the setup stroke as normal.

Make the sweep by reaching your arm and rod far away from you toward the far bank and certainly not in a vertical plane.

This will allow the fly line to land on the water much farther away from you than the vertical sweep did.

See how far the line has landed away from me? With the right pirouette and line speed on the D-loop stroke, it will automatically result in a smaller D loop.

Fault Finding

1 **It is impossible to get the nail knot to land in the correct position at the end of the setup stroke.** If the tip of your fly line lands upstream of you, stop the cast. Completing the cast will only end up with your forward stroke crossing the rail track and the fly snagging you, the rod, or the line. This is caused by too fast a setup stroke. Either start the rod higher before you make the setup stroke, or slow down your setup stroke. If the line stays too far downstream of you at the end of the setup stroke, you have either made too slow a stroke or started the rod too high.

The correct position of the line tip at the end of the setup stroke is directly in line with where you want to aim your forward stroke.

Too fast a setup stroke will make the line and leader fly out of the water and finish lying upstream of you. This cast, completed to the original target (X), will cross the rail track and tangle.

Too slow a setup stroke and the line tip will land a long way downstream of your target (you can tell by the ripples). You have to change your target (to X) or you will get a bloody L anchor and have a bad case of dribbly front loop.

2 **Bloody L Anchor.** As with all change-of-direction casts, you can put the dreaded bloody L into the anchor prior to the forward stroke. As always, this is not the route to success. With the double spey there are a couple of causes of the bloody L: If you make too slow a setup stroke and the line tip lands a long way downstream of you, you will get the bloody L. Remember, the perfect place for the nail knot at the end of the setup stroke is directly in line with your target. If you make any kind of dip with the tip of the rod on the D-loop stroke, you will certainly put in a bloody L. Keep the rod tip rising throughout the entire D-loop stroke. If you have too slow a D-loop stroke and don't impart enough speed in the line to make it pirouette at the very tip, you will end up with a bloody L.

If you make too slow a D-loop stroke, you will not give the line enough speed to rotate the line from an upstream/downstream plane to a lined-up-with-the-target plane. The line that has not swung into the correct plane leaves a bloody L.

A bloody L anchor will always be the result if you make a dip with the rod tip in the D-loop stroke. Keep the rod tip rising smoothly all the way around to the key position to avoid this.

3 **The line comes out of the water when the D-loop stroke is made.** Speed kills! Either you have made the D-loop stroke with too much speed or the rod has made too sharp an incline, lifting the line out of the water and neatly depositing it in the bushes behind.

If the line comes out of the water when you make the D-loop stroke, you may have had too much speed in the D-loop stroke.

The rod may have had too steep an incline throughout the D-loop stroke. Keep the incline at a nice gentle angle of about 25 degrees.

4 The forward loop has no speed as it goes out, even though the rail track and timing were (apparently) correct. It might also collide and have a bit of a tangle. As always, the D loop needs to be opposite where you make the forward stroke. A common problem with the double spey is putting too much speed at the start of the D-loop stroke. This sends the momentum of the D loop more downstream than behind. Try holding any speed off the D-loop stroke until you start to bring the rod back in toward the bank you are standing on and opposite where you actually want the forward cast to go.

If you put any speed in the first part of the D-loop stroke, you will put the D loop's momentum downstream and away from you and the target line. This does not load the rod correctly and will result in a poor forward cast, if aimed across the river, and maybe even a collision loop.

Ideally, there should be a slight increase in speed during the D-loop stroke, but only in a direction opposite your target. By holding that slight increase in power until the latter stage of the D-loop stroke, you will send the D loop more behind you and opposite the target, which will load the rod more deeply and efficiently.

In the traditional world of spey casting, with two-handed rods, the classic two casts are the single spey and the double spey, which have been around since the mid-1800s. As more people have gotten into the game of spey casting, more casts have been developed, and some of these modern casts are particularly cool with a single-handed rod. The next part of the book delves into some of these more modern spey casts.

CHAPTER 11

The Snake Roll

Continuous Motion Group
Airborne Anchor Subgroup

The snake roll is another cast that falls into the spey family. Like all the other spey casts, its primary use is to make a change-of-direction cast with obstacles behind. Before you go any further in this book, look at the previous chapter (Double Spey) and the summaries of when to use this cast and hand to use, and compare them to the ones shown here. You'll find them the same! Like the double spey, the snake roll uses the same hand during the same conditions.

So, why do you need another cast that does exactly the same thing as the double spey? Logically you don't. If you can make a single spey and a double spey and make both casts with some degree of proficiency from either side of your body, you are set and can fish in any situation with any wind direction.

However, there are a couple of aspects that give the snake roll an advantage. First, it is a faster change of direction, meaning less time casting, more time fishing. It is also a cast that keeps the rod and line on one side of your body all the time. This is good if you are fishing in tight situations and have little space to swing a cat in, never mind a fly rod. Another difference between the double spey and snake roll is the subgroup. The snake roll has an airborne anchor, the double spey a waterborne anchor. Once you have made a few of both casts you will see the significance in this, but the main thing this means is that the snake roll is deadly quiet whereas the double spey makes a sloshing, tearing sound as the waterborne anchor is unstuck from the water. On calm pools in the first light of a summer's morn and with fish selectively supping duns in the margins, you want a nice quiet cast. If those aren't reasons enough to make you want to learn another cast, how about fun! This is a fun cast. It is fun to whiz your line back and forth, changing direction here, there, and everywhere without being concerned about snagging your flies. Sold? I hope so!

When to use this cast: changes of direction, obstructions behind, wind blowing downstream.
Hand to use: Right hand for a direction change to the left, left hand (or backhand) for a direction change to the right.

How this cast came about is a unique story. In short, it was a cast I developed in the 1980s when teaching casting with my dad in Devon, England. The cast came about by accident as I was bumming around, flicking fly line around on the river one day, merging a couple of roll casts into one. My dad was videotaping me doing this, and it wasn't until we were watching the playback that we saw it as a cast with potential. I wanted to call it the sausage roll but my dad argued his point about a sensible name, and the snake roll was born. To be fair, I have seen many casters flicking their lines around in the same sort of way. You just develop an enjoyment of casting and fiddle around with stuff. Many people have made snake rolls without knowing this name—before and after I was playing around on the River Torridge—but the name seems to have stuck.

Anyway, enough history, on to physics!

The snake roll has an airborne anchor, so timing is always going to be more critical than with the double spey. Like the single spey and switch cast before, this requires the splash-and-go approach, but before we get to the forward stroke and the timing, let's look at how you make the D-loop stroke. (Being a member of the airborne anchor subgroup means there is no setup stroke.)

The D-loop stroke is a little unusual. Unlike the previous casts that have fairly straight rod tip paths and an obvious casting stroke to form the D loop, the snake roll has a corkscrewing, twisting move that relies on torque to position the anchor.

The rod tip prescribes a rather large letter e shape for the D-loop stroke. If you are making a cast with your right hand (changing direction to the left), it is a normal e, counterclockwise in direction. For a change of direction to the right (with the left hand, or a backhanded, right-handed cast), it is a reverse e, clockwise in direction.

Every continuous motion cast you make has to have a rising rod tip at the end of the D-loop stroke. This is to ensure that you keep the lower leg of the D loop from falling into the water and sticking in the surface film. So to complete the shape of the D-loop stroke, you finish the e by raising the rod to the key position.

You start the e slowly, dragging the rod tip level and back toward the bank you are fishing from, and then accelerate through the curves of the e and up to the key position. Accelerating doesn't mean going at full pelt! Acceleration is just an increase of speed. Most people whip through this e with too much speed. The acceleration should be smooth and gradual.

While the e is a good picture to have, I find that it can be a little disorientating just to say, "Draw an e shape." A final part of the analogy is to imagine your rod tip has a piece of chalk jammed in the end and that you are drawing the e shape on a brick wall. The rod tip must not come off the wall while you draw the shape, even when lifting to the key position.

Another thing to remember about the e is that it should be large and fluid. Don't be ashamed of your snake—draw it as big as you can and make sure you generate enough torque to flip the fly, leader, and fly line from a downstream position to the rail track, aligned with your target position. As you get better at this, you can make smaller and more efficient strokes, but without having the feel, don't start this way. Keep it big!

One useful bonus of the wall analogy is that the rail track will always (if done right) land pointing in a parallel plane to the wall. In other words, wherever you want to aim your forward stroke, make sure you have your imaginary wall running in that direction, and draw the shape along that plane.

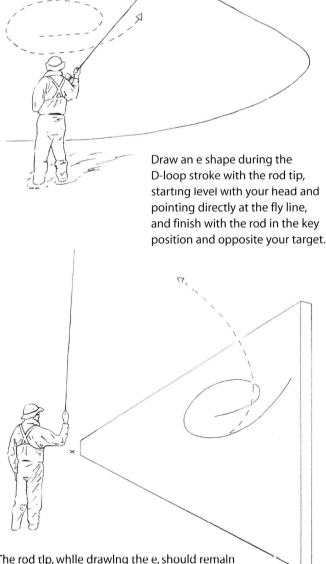

Draw an e shape during the D-loop stroke with the rod tip, starting level with your head and pointing directly at the fly line, and finish with the rod in the key position and opposite your target.

The rod tip, while drawing the e, should remain on one plane, as though there was a piece of chalk wedged in the end and you were drawing the shape on a brick wall. Do not allow the rod tip to leave this wall during the D-loop stroke.

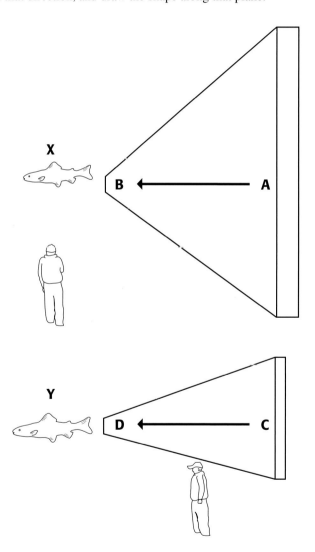

For accuracy, picture the brick wall running in the direction of your target and keep the rod tip on that plane. To cast at X, I would picture my brick wall running along AB, and to cast to Y my brick wall runs along CD.

The snake roll starts with the line tight and the rod level, pointing directly at the fly and about the height of your head.

The first move of the snake roll is a slow, smooth, level drag of the rod back behind you.

Without a pause, start to raise the rod and accelerate smoothly through the beginning of an e shape.

The rod reaches its highest point, still accelerating and continuing the e shape. The highest point is not above you, but to the side, remaining on the brick wall.

The rod starts to come down from the highest point and reaches in front of you, accelerating slightly, though still on the wall.

The rod reaches the lowest point of the e shape (about head height) and starts to pull back to create a D loop. At this point all the fly line should be in the air.

The rod tip has leveled out and remains at head height as it passes you.

The rod rises to the key position and gets there before any fly line has landed on the water.

The rod stays motionless in the key position as you watch the line tip head toward the water.

The moment the fly line (or leader) touches the water, the forward stroke commences.

A perfect cast can only result from a forward stroke that is parallel and close to the anchor.

A high, crisp stop of the rod will result in a perfect loop that unrolls in the air.

Like all casts, you should be able to make a snake roll from either side of your body. Sometimes you will need to change direction to the left and sometimes to the right. As always, you can either switch hands and alternate between right and left hand, or just keep to your dominant hand and cast backhanded for the other side (a reverse snake roll). Just remember that when you change direction to the left, using your right hand, you draw a regular e shape, counterclockwise in direction. To change direction to the right (the left-handed version), you need to make a reverse, mirror-image e, clockwise. Here's a series of photos illustrating the left-handed snake roll.

Start the rod low, pointing toward the fly line, and begin by pushing it back toward the bank behind you.

Begin to accelerate slightly and bring the rod tip up toward a vertical plane but still keep it on the proverbial brick wall.

Continue sweeping the rod out in front of you clockwise and then down level with your shoulder and back toward the bank you are standing near.

Finish the D-loop stroke with an acceleration, lifting the rod to the key position before any fly line or leader has touched the water.

Pause in the key position until the first piece of fly line or leader touches the water.

When it does, immediately drive the forward stroke out parallel to the anchor lying on the water.

Watch the loop sail out to where you want it to go—a change-of-direction cast from your left side to the right.

If you really want to nail this cast, I suggest practicing it in a pond, calm ocean bay, or slow-moving piece of river. Stand in the middle and make a snake roll from your right-hand side to the left with your right hand. Then make a direction change from where it landed, putting the line back where it started, using the left hand or a reverse snake roll.

Keep doing this and develop a rhythm of the cast in either direction, so when the situation arises, you don't have to stop and think, "Now which direction should my rod go?"

Even though the photos and descriptions emphasize the use of a snake roll in a river where there are obstructions behind and for people who like to swing a fly across the current, don't get it stuck in your head that this is the only time to make a snake roll. Indeed, there is no faster, more accurate or efficient a change-of-direction cast than this. I use the snake roll (and reverse snake roll) constantly when fishing a river with a dry fly to a casual supping trout, or on a lake when targeting a rising or cruising fish, and indeed, there is no better cast on a bonefish flat where I need a quick change-of-direction cast to get my fly in front of a fast-traveling bonefish.

Once you master this cast, you will discover how many opportunities (and fish) it opens up.

Fault Finding

1 **The fly line does not come out of the water when the D-loop stroke has been completed, but stays where it started.** There are a number of causes for this frustrating problem. If the line is slack at the start of the cast, and before you draw the e shape, you will never get the line to leave its starting position and create a good rail track. More commonly the problem is that the e has no acceleration to generate the torque needed to get the line out of the water. Make sure you accelerate the rod a little as the rod rounds the e and starts to rise to the key position. Failure to get the line out of the water is also caused by a pause somewhere in the e, as the brain tries to analyze the moves. Once you start the e, the rod should never pause or slow down until it gets into the key position.

When the rod is in the key position, the line should have come cleanly out of the water and created a rail track that is pointing directly toward the target.

If there is slack in the line to start, or the e shape is too slow or has a pause in it, the line will fail to get out of the water and stay stuck downstream of you, with no rail track to the target.

2 "I can't get my rail track to line up with my target." This very common problem is caused by either your imaginary brick wall running in the wrong direction (not toward the target), or by the rod coming off the wall during the D-loop stroke.

If my target is AB and the fly line has landed here (CD) and I continue my forward cast toward B, the cast will fail. Usually this is caused by the rod tip coming off the imaginary brick wall, or because the brick wall is running in the wrong direction.

3 "I keep hitting myself with the fly line as I make my forward stroke." This is another problem caused by the rod tip coming off the brick wall, this time as the rod lifts to the key position. I call this a secondary move. Most people find it strange to make a casting stroke with the rod held at such an angle and keeping in touch with the brick wall; they want to lift the rod up close to their ear for the key position. This extra movement—pulling the rod off the wall and close to the ear—pulls the D loop off the plane and toward you. As you make the forward stroke, the line hits the body.

A successful cast comes from the rod traveling in directly opposing planes—keeping the D-loop stroke and forward stroke opposite each other. By pulling the rod off the plane that you started the D loop on and toward the ear, the line and D loop itself are dragged close to you. Sometimes it will hit you, sometimes it won't, but it will always have a miserable forward cast!

4 "When I start the forward stroke, the line collapses in front of me." Assuming that the forward stroke itself is correct, this can only be caused by a poorly timed forward stroke. Too long a pause between the D-loop stroke and the forward stroke results in too much line on the water, and the line sticks in the water surface film. Too early a forward cast and there is not enough anchor to grip the line and ensure the D loop has tension. As a result, the rod has no load and the cast collapses in the water in front.

If you pause too long between the D loop and forward stroke, too much line will land on the water, creating an excessive anchor. This extra drag takes all the energy out of the forward cast and makes the line dribble out ineffectively. A telltale sign of this is a loud slurp or spray sound as the line tries to rip out of the gluey meniscus.

So there we have it, a fairly short chapter compared with the single and double spey ones, but by this stage, if you have done all your homework and muscle memory exercises, you really shouldn't need a 5,000-word chapter to get the basics dialed in. The better you get, the less information you need to learn something new, and by now you should have a good understanding of the basics.

CHAPTER 12

The Snap T

Continuous Motion Group
Waterborne Anchor Subgroup

Just as the snake roll is an alternative cast to the double spey, the snap T is an alternative cast for the single spey. As before, you really don't need to learn the snap T as well as the single spey—they do the some sort of thing, are used in the same conditions, and have the same direction change.

Again, though, it is pretty cool to be competent at a wide range of casts, and adding the snap T to your repertoire is pretty satisfying.

Apart from that satisfaction, the snap T definitely has a couple of advantages over the single spey:It is generally easier to learn, and as part of the waterborne anchor group of casts, it is much more efficient at throwing big flies, weight, and (if you need to) sink tips.

Let me explain that second point in a little more detail. One thing to keep reminding yourself is that the water is a grip—it holds any fly line that is lying on it in its meniscus. This grip is not necessarily a bad thing. If you have an unbalanced rig (big flies, heavy flies, indicators, weight . . . that sort of unbalanced rig), the grip of the water is actually a good thing and prevents the line from kicking when it is being cast. If you make an airborne anchor cast, the fly/sink tip/indicator/weight is traveling back through the air on the D-loop stroke and has to reverse its

> **When to use this cast:** changes of direction, obstructions behind, wind blowing upstream.
> **Hand to use:** Right hand for a direction change to the right, left hand (or backhand) for a direction change to the left.

direction to go forward. The unbalanced outfit is prone to kick and protest at such treatment. With the waterborne anchor casts, the grip of the line in the water stops the aggressive kick because the line is not traveling back through the air; it remains on the water. Thus, the group of waterborne anchor casts will always give smoother and more efficient casts with unbalanced outfits. Because the snap T has a waterborne anchor, it is definitely the cast of choice when using such gear.

The snap T is a cast with a number of subtle variations and names. The cast is also called the snap C, the circle C, the snap Z, the C spey, and the circle spey. The names are different, and the initial setup stroke of each cast is slightly different. After the setup stroke, each of these variations are principally the same, and to avoid confusion, I teach my students one version and one name—keep life simple!

The snap T is a cast that consists of three strokes. Just like the double spey, it has a setup stroke, D-loop stroke, and forward stroke. I have found that the fastest way to learn this cast is to master it step by step. Just work on the setup stroke alone, and don't worry about the D-loop stroke until you can competently and confidently snap the line into the correct position for the D-loop stroke.

Setup Stroke

As in all setup strokes, the object is to position the line in the correct place to aid an efficient D loop and rail track. This is achieved by ensuring that the tip of the fly line lands pretty well in line (or just upstream) of your target line. As usual, I want to describe the how-to of this cast as if you were on a river with the current flowing from right to left (the left bank, looking downstream) and for a right-handed caster.

The cast starts with the line washed straight and tight directly downstream of you with the rod tip low and pointing along the fly line.

Begin the setup stroke with a slow, steady vertical lift of the rod up to about 11 o'clock, and then make a wide, clockwise curve of the rod tip back to the starting point. This is a large D shape. The lift really does need to be vertical—don't be tempted to lift with a diagonal rise of the rod tip. There is no pause in the D; once you have started the lift, continue to draw the D shape with the rod tip until the tip of the rod is back to where it started.

What you are trying to do with this D shape is pick up the line, leader, and fly and snap it into a position that is upstream of you and your target. To do this you actually need a slight acceleration in the bottom part of the D.

There must be a pause between the end of the setup stroke and the start of the D-loop stroke. Use this pause to find where the tip of the fly line has landed, as this will indicate where the rail track will be set and where the most efficient forward cast should be aimed.

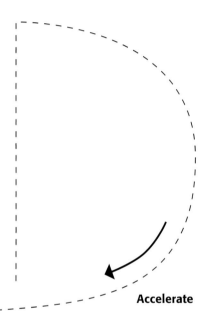

The first part of the snap T cast is the setup stroke. Draw a large D shape with the tip of the rod. The D must have some acceleration in the lower part of the shape, right where the thicker arrow starts.

Accelerate

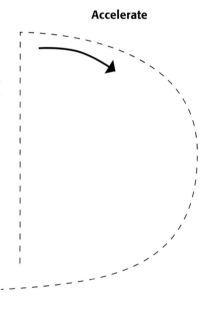

Many casters start accelerating too early, as in this D. Make sure you wait until the rod is traveling almost horizontally, back toward the starting position, before beginning the acceleration.

Accelerate

The setup stroke starts with the fly line washed downstream and a low rod tip that is pointing along the fly line.

Lift the rod smoothly and slowly in a vertical plane to about 11 o'clock, still pointing downstream.

Without a pause, but again smoothly, start to draw a clockwise directional curve with the rod tip (for the right-handed cast).

The clockwise D shape brings the rod down toward the water and back on a horizontal plane. At this stage the line has momentum and has all lifted out of the water.

The rod completes the D shape with a slight acceleration (snap) and finishes back where it started. The fly line is still airborne and traveling in a curve past you.

Wait with the rod completely still and low while the fly line continues its path upstream.

D-Loop Stroke

The D-loop stroke is the same here as with the double spey. If you have done the setup stroke correctly, the rod tip should finish in a low position close to the water (about a foot from the surface is fine) and pointing downstream. The fly line should be in an up-stream/downstream plane and the fly and leader just upstream of you.

The rod tip should now make the D-loop stroke, sweeping around to the key position with a steady incline and a constant speed. The incline should not be steep—an angle of about 20 degrees is ideal—and the finishing point of this inclined sweep is with the rod tip about 1 o'clock and directly opposite your intended target.

The sweep speed should just be enough to pirouette the whole line around the line tip (just as I described with the double spey) and align a perfect rail track to your target. As with the double spey, too slow a sweep (or a dreaded dip) will result in only part of the line swiveling and a bloody L. Too fast a sweep (or too steep), and the line will lift out of the water and into the nearest tree!

The ideal D-loop stroke repositions the line from an upstream/downstream position (where it has landed on the setup stroke) to a perfect rail track to your target. For this to succeed, you need enough speed in the rod sweep to put the right amount of momentum into the fly line to break the water surface tension and allow it to line up with your target.

Once all the fly line, leader, and the fly has landed, start the second stroke, the D-loop stroke.

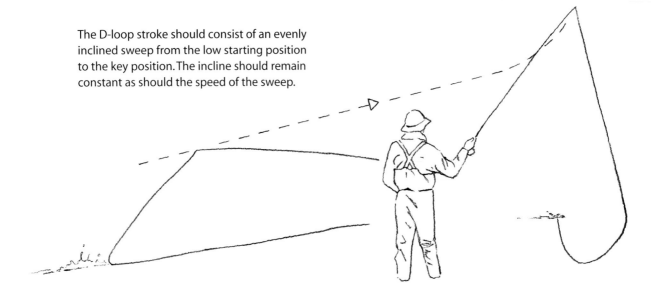

The D-loop stroke should consist of an evenly inclined sweep from the low starting position to the key position. The incline should remain constant as should the speed of the sweep.

The rod tip travels on a slight incline of 20 degrees or so throughout the D-loop stroke. There should be enough speed in this stroke to start to tear the fly line out of the water.

The D-loop stroke continues with the rod tip still rising until the rod is just about opposite the target.

The D-loop stroke finishes with the rod rising to the key position and directly opposite where the target is. Here you must wait until the entire D loop has stopped moving before commencing the forward stroke.

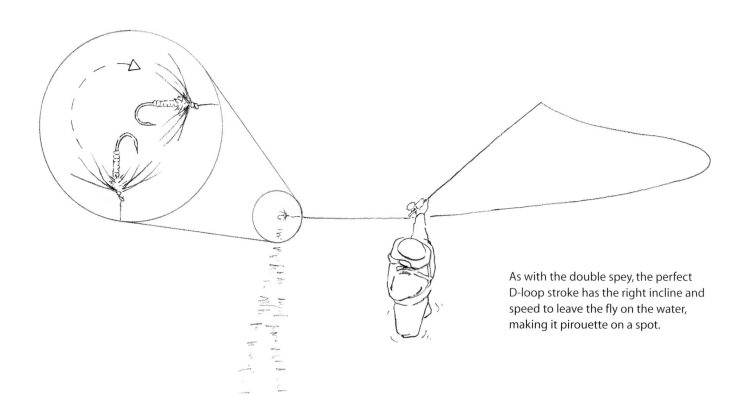

As with the double spey, the perfect D-loop stroke has the right incline and speed to leave the fly on the water, making it pirouette on a spot.

The Forward Stroke

A D loop has three stages of movement: the travel, the stop, and the drop. When the rod has made a D-loop stroke, it imparts momentum into the line that makes the D loop travel backwards, behind you (the travel). At some stage, the D loop will run out of momentum, stop traveling (the stop) and then drop down onto the water (the drop). The perfect timing of the forward cast on all waterborne anchor casts is when the D loop reaches the stop. If you go forward when there is still momentum in the D loop (the travel), the two forces (backwards of the D loop and forwards of the forward stroke) will make the line rip out of the water, losing the anchor and stability of the cast and ensuring that the line falls in a heap in front. If you wait marginally too long and allow the D loop to drop to the water, there will be too much line stick and drag and all the energy of the cast will be sucked out by the water tension. Some people find it helpful to stand at a sideways angle and watch their D loop travel backwards, watching it until it stops and then timing the forward cast perfectly.

All that remains now is to finish off with a good forward stroke, driving a tight loop through the air, close to, and parallel to, the rail track. The correct length of pause between the completion of the D-loop stroke and the start of the forward stroke depends on many factors—line length, fly size, rod length, and wading depth, to name a few—but the precise time to start the forward stroke is when the D loop stops traveling backwards.

When the D-loop stroke has finished, the fly line lying on the water has rotated and is fully lined up with the target, and the D loop has stopped traveling backwards, the forward stroke starts—aiming directly along the rail tracks.

By stopping the rod tip high and with a positive stop, you form a tight front loop that will keep the cast effortless and efficient.

Keep the rod tip high and still as the loop unrolls, and lower the rod only when the fly line starts to fall toward the water surface. This will ensure the loop stays nice and tight and the line will land with perfect presentation.

A very common problem to avoid when making the D-loop stroke is dipping the rod tip during this stroke. A smooth incline of about 20 degrees and with no dip in the rod tip is perfect. Should you dip the rod tip, be too slow with the stroke, or have too flat a D-loop stroke, you will end up with the dreaded bloody L in the fly line. This will never give a good forward cast.

If the D-loop stroke is too slow, the incline too shallow, or the rod has a slight dip in the sweep, a bloody L will result.

I have described the snap T cast here for right-handed casters—changing the line's position from their left-hand side to their right-hand side. To make a left-handed (or a backhanded) cast and change the line's position from the right side of the body to the left (as though you were standing in a river with the current flowing from left to right), you need to make only one change—change the D shape to a C shape. In other words, make a counterclockwise curve of the rod, not a clockwise one. Other than that, the cast is identical.

From the other side of the river, or to change the line's position from your right-hand side to the left, you will need to make a left-handed cast (or a right-handed cast from the backhand side).

Reverse the D shape to a counterclockwise C shape.

Like the right-handed snap T, the finish of the rod tip position on the setup stroke is low, close to the water, and pointing back at where the rod tip started. The rest of the cast is identical to the right-handed version described above.

Fault Finding

1 "The fly line does not come out of the water when I make the setup stroke." Assuming your line is tight and straight at the start of the cast, there are a couple of reasons for this failure. It could be because the initial lift has not been high enough to unstick a decent amount of fly line for the D shape to be effective. It could be because there has been a pause at the top of the lift and before the start of the curve shape, allowing the fly line to drop back and settle in the water. However, the most likely reason is the acceleration or snap of the setup stroke has either not been in the horizontal plane, or there just hasn't been enough of a snap to get the line to kick out.

If you find at the end of the setup stroke that the line and leader have not come out of the water but are still somewhere downstream of you, it is wrong and dangerous to complete the cast. This failure to get the line tip out of the water and land just upstream of you is possibly caused by a lift that is not high enough at the start of the cast.

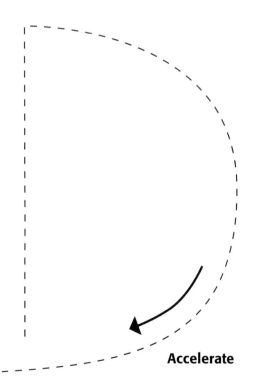

It is probably because there is no snap in the lower part of the D. Remember, you should accelerate the D in the lower horizontal section.

Accelerate

2 It is impossible to get the line tip to land in the correct position at the end of the setup stroke. As you get better at the snap T, you try to land the line tip pretty well in line with your target. Too far upstream of your target and you will have diverging rail tracks and the line will run out of energy. Too far downstream of your target and you will cross the rail track (if you still aim at the target) and tangle. The plane that you draw the D shape on is the major influence of the line tip's landing position. Imagine two brick walls, one running directly in front of you in an up-stream/downstream plane and the other running 90 degrees to that on your left-hand side, running in an across-stream plane. If you draw your D shape on the front wall, you will always land your line tip upstream of you. If you draw your D shape on the side wall, on your downstream shoulder, you will rarely land the line tip upstream of you. Both planes can be correct; which wall you draw your D shape on determines where your most effective forward cast should be aimed.

As a student of casting, you need to be able to control the landing point of your line tip at the end of the setup stroke, so play around with where your theoretical wall is and see how it affects this position.

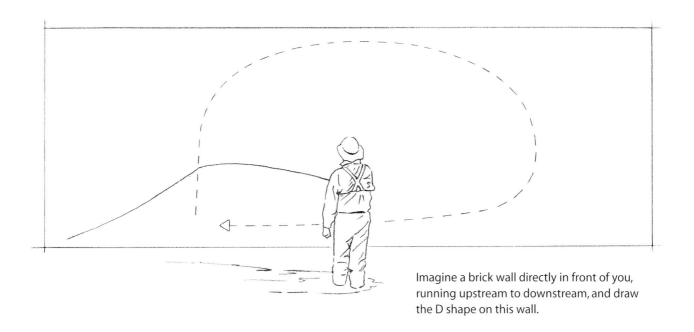

Imagine a brick wall directly in front of you, running upstream to downstream, and draw the D shape on this wall.

You will always land your line tip upstream of you.

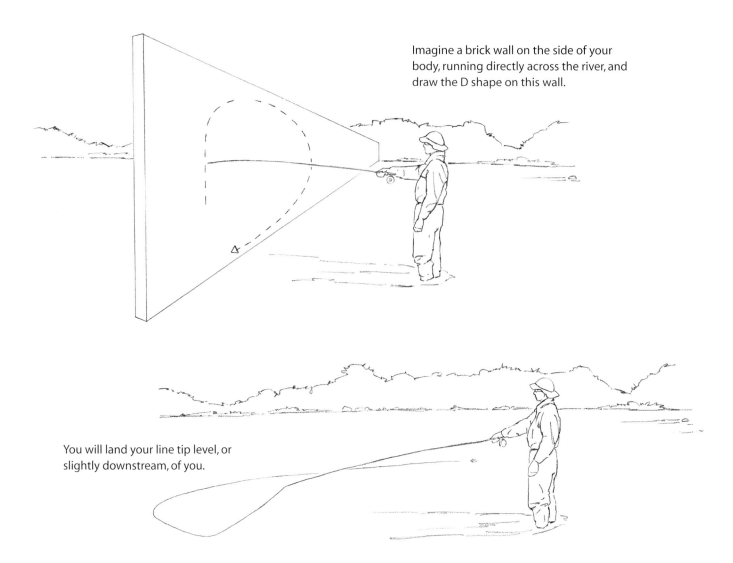

Imagine a brick wall on the side of your body, running directly across the river, and draw the D shape on this wall.

You will land your line tip level, or slightly downstream, of you.

Make the rod tip path of the initial setup stroke as though you were drawing it on a wall that is directly in front of you (parallel to the river flow) …

…and you will ensure the line tip lands upstream of you. This is fine if you want to make your cast upstream of where you are standing—toward the line tip lying on the water. Just adjust the aiming point of your forward stroke to compensate for this.

Draw the D shape on a side wall (perpendicular to the current) …

…and you will ensure the line tip lands just downstream of you. This is fine if you want to make your cast at a fine angle and not at 90 degrees of where you are standing.

3 **"Bloody L" anchor.** Just like the double spey, there are a couple of causes of the bloody L. If you throw your line tip too far upstream of your target on the setup stroke and then make the D-loop stroke as if you were still aiming at that target, you will get a bloody L. If you make any kind of dip with the tip of the rod on the D-loop stroke, you will certainly put in a bloody L—keep the rod tip rising throughout the entire D-loop stroke until you get to the key position. If you have too slow a D-loop stroke and don't impart enough momentum to make the line tip pirouette, you will end up with a bloody L.

A snap that lays the line tip a long way upstream of your target line, and a D-loop stroke still aimed opposite the target, will result in bloody L.

If you dip the rod at all in the D-loop stroke, you will always get a bloody L. Keep the rod tip rising smoothly all the way around to the key position.

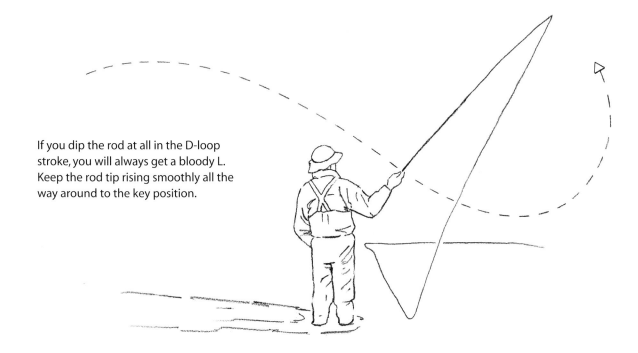

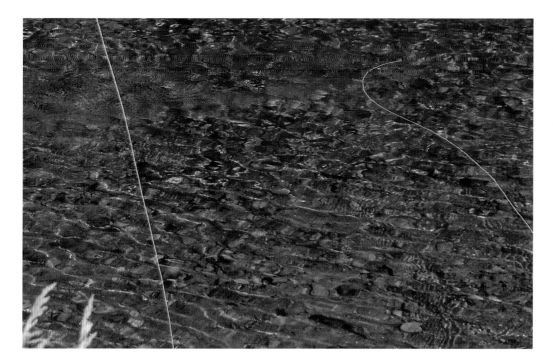

A slow D-loop stroke will not impart enough speed to rotate the line from an upstream/downstream plane to a lined-up-with-the-target plane. This will leave a bloody L.

4 **The line comes out of the water when I make the D-loop stroke.** Either you have made the D-loop stroke with too much speed or the rod has made too sharp an incline. Keep the speed constant and smooth and the incline subtle.

The line tip and leader should never come out of the water during the D-loop stroke. If they do, it is because either there was too much speed in the D-loop stroke or the rod had too steep an incline throughout the D-loop stroke. Keep the incline at a nice, gentle angle of about 30 degrees.

As I mentioned at the beginning of this chapter, this cast has a number of variations, and it is nice to know, and be able to perform, all of them. However, master this version first, and then experiment and play and see where it leads.

CHAPTER 13

The Dry-Fly Spey

To-and-Fro and Continuous Motion Groups
Airborne Anchor Subgroup

The dry-fly spey is unique in that it is the only cast that is a combination of both a to-and-fro cast and a continuous motion cast. You can use an overhead cast or a side cast as the to-and-fro cast and a single spey or a snake roll as the continuous motion cast.

I used this cast, and indeed developed it, on the Bray, my home river in Devon. The river is narrow and overgrown, with deep holes that prevent an angler from wading out. (Spooky moorland sea trout also make it a bad idea to wade out!) You are frequently tucked up tight to the bank, trying to cast a dry fly

When to use this cast: changes of direction, obstructions behind, fishing a dry fly.

across the river. You certainly can't make a regular overhead cast across the river because the bushes are too thick behind you, and while you could make one or two successful spey casts across the river with your dry fly, any more than that result in the fly becoming waterlogged and (with no false casts to dry the feathers off) remaining waterlogged and useless.

It is another of the casts that I am sure many anglers develop to get out of a situation similar to the ones I would find on the Bray. I am sure this cast has other names, but I always called it the dry-fly spey.

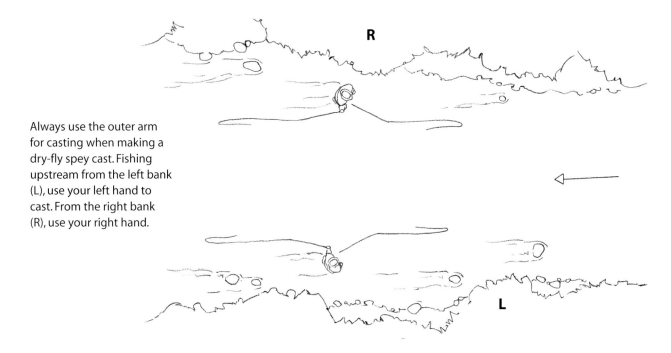

Always use the outer arm for casting when making a dry-fly spey cast. Fishing upstream from the left bank (L), use your left hand to cast. From the right bank (R), use your right hand.

This cast is always performed with the casting hand that is farthest from the riverbank. If you are standing on the left bank of the river fishing upstream (trees on your right-hand side), use your left hand; on the right bank (fishing upstream), use your right hand. If you are fishing downstream, use the opposite hand.

The cast starts with an ordinary overhead cast, aiming the false casts directly upstream and downstream and where there are no trees. If there are overhanging trees, use the side cast, but again aim upstream and downstream and parallel to the river bank. These false casts are to dry the fly. Once the fly is dry, you make your final forward cast a little higher than normal, let the loop unroll and, when the line is straight and before it drops to the water, make a single spey.

It is important to time the single spey right and make the final forward stroke with only the minimum of pauses. If you make your false casts, dry the fly, and then have a long pause after the D-loop stroke of the single spey, the dry fly will sit on the water too long and get waterlogged, negating the usefulness of this cast.

The Bray, in North Devon, is my home river and one of the rivers I will always list in my top five places in the world to fish. I used the dry-fly spey cast here more than at any other venue because of the overhanging trees and super spooky fish.

Start the dry fly spey with the outermost hand — the one that is nearest the middle of the river.

Make false casts directly upstream and downstream, drying the fly. If you have space, use an overhead cast. If you have overhanging trees, use the side cast.

When the fly is dry, make the final forward cast angled slightly higher and let the loop unroll completely.

Immediately dip the rod into the D-loop stroke of the single spey.

Rotate your rod and body so that the rod finishes in the key position directly opposite where you want your forward cast to go. Also, make sure that the line that lands on the water leaves room for your forward stroke without crossing the line—remember the rail tracks.

Make your forward stroke toward the target, ensuring that you start the forward stroke at the earliest moment.

Watch your fly land two feet upstream of the fish, drift naturally toward it, and be engulfed by that 20-inch brown that nobody has ever been able to catch!

Here's another way of looking at this cast, this time with Greg's illustrations.

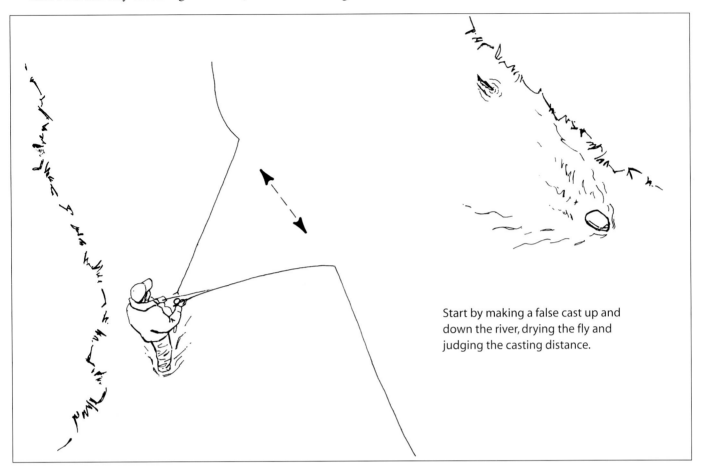

Start by making a false cast up and down the river, drying the fly and judging the casting distance.

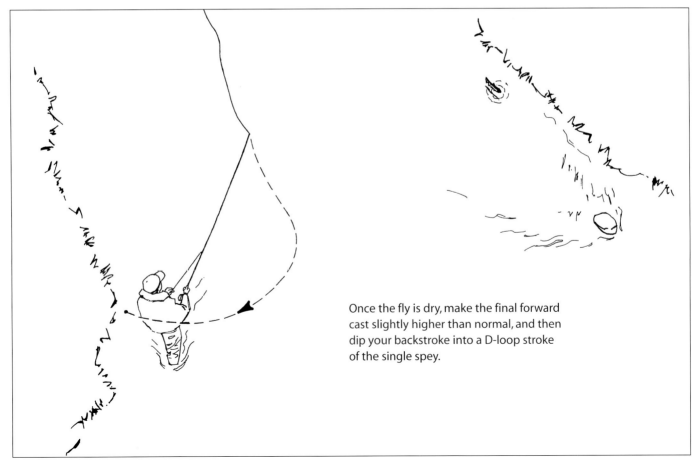

Once the fly is dry, make the final forward cast slightly higher than normal, and then dip your backstroke into a D-loop stroke of the single spey.

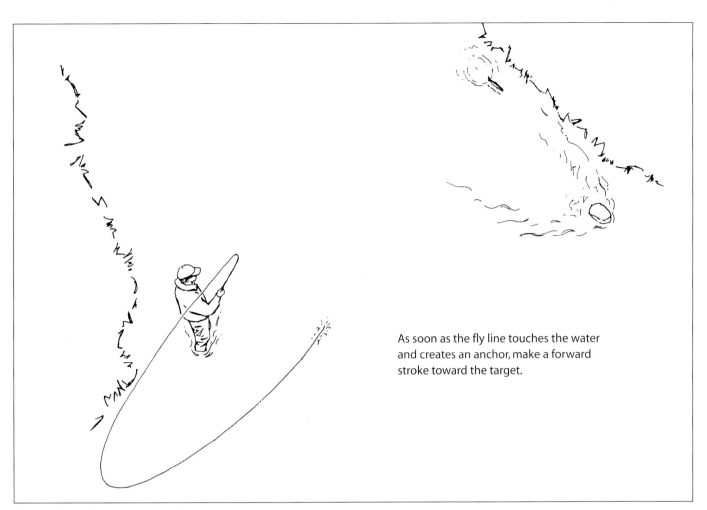

As soon as the fly line touches the water and creates an anchor, make a forward stroke toward the target.

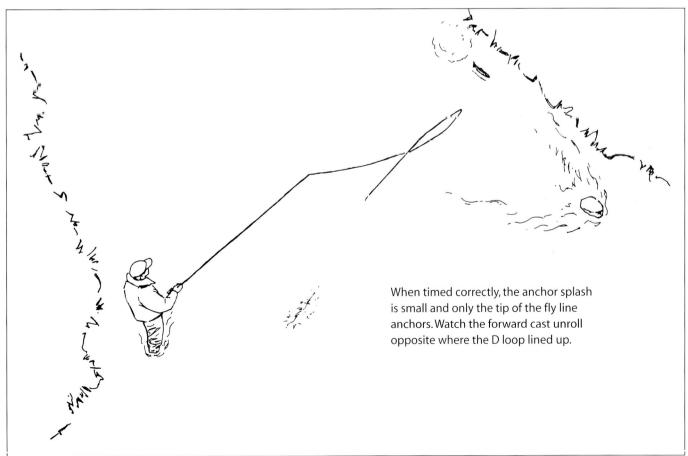

When timed correctly, the anchor splash is small and only the tip of the fly line anchors. Watch the forward cast unroll opposite where the D loop lined up.

The dry-fly spey is pretty useless on its own. You also have to know the dry-fly spey pickup, which, fortunately, is easy if you've gotten this far in your casting prowess!

If your fly is across the river and you need to recast, do not pick up the fly with a regular overhead cast—not if there are bushes behind you—you'll end up closely examining exactly what leaves are on the tree! Instead use a snake roll to pick up the line, aiming the forward stroke directly upstream and, before it lands, smoothly continuing into a series of false casts to dry off the fly again. Continue this mix of dry-fly spey and dry-fly spey pickup until you have caught all the fish in the pool (or at least until you catch the one fish you are after).

I use the single spey here as an illustration and to keep it relatively simple. However, you could also make the dry-fly spey with a snake roll, which is a little more effective at wider angle changes. The only downside with the snake roll version of the dry-fly spey is that you have to use your inside arm to make the cast—the one nearest the bushes—and sometimes you won't have room for that.

Without the dry-fly spey pickup, the regular dry-fly spey will be useless. With a tree behind and a fly line in front, a normal overhead cast will just throw the carefully dried fly into the tree. Use a snake roll to pick up the line from the water. Start by dragging the rod low and behind you.

Start the initial snake roll forward loop, in a counterclockwise direction, with the rod tip.

Pull the rod back on the D-loop stroke while the fly line is still in the air.

Raise the rod into the key position with a little added speed, as you do not want it to land on the water and create an anchor.

You should have enough acceleration to create a regular backcast and straighten the line in the air behind you. Before any fly line, or the leader, touches the water, smoothly start the forward stroke.

Aim opposite the D loop.

Watch the line unroll—safe from any obstructions behind!

PROBLEMS IN FRONT

CHAPTER 14

The Side Cast

To-and-Fro Group

The side cast isn't strictly a new cast; at least not if you can make a reasonably good overhead cast. It is just an overhead cast turned onto a horizontal plane.

You might ask what use this is. Well, there isn't a use, not in the singular sense of the word anyway—there are several uses. If you need to make a forward cast underneath an obstacle, you would use a side cast; if you need to keep your backcast underneath an obstacle, you would use a side cast;

When to use this cast: Any situation that requires casting the fly line low and horizontal, close to the water.

if you want a feather-soft presentation, you would use a side cast; if you want to bend your fly line around something, you would use a side cast. In other words, the side cast is a pretty useful tool, particularly to the small-stream fly fisher.

One thing the side cast is not is a distance cast. The fact that your fly line travels only a couple of feet above the water makes it impossible to get any distance or carry long lengths of line.

The side cast has many uses; probably the most common is when you are faced with an overhanging tree and need to get your fly underneath—hopefully because there is a large fish there!

You can also use a side cast when you have wide open spaces in front and an obstacle behind.

Another great use of the side cast is to get a super-soft landing of the fly. With your front loop traveling so close to the water and only dropping a foot to land, it is a great cast when presentation is vital.

Yet one more use of this cast is when you need to bend the end of your fly line and get it to land with a curve. On its own the side cast will not do this, but knowing this cast makes it possible. More on this bent cast later.

As I said at the beginning of this chapter, the side cast is just an overhead cast turned on its side. The first step of this cast is to turn the rod sideways so that the reel is flat, parallel to the water, and the rod guides are facing your intended forward cast. If you are making a forehand, or regular side, cast (with either hand) your knuckles should be facing down toward the ground and thumb opposite your forward cast. For a backhanded cast, reverse the grip so your knuckles are facing up, but again the thumb is opposite the intended forward cast. As in all casts, the line needs to be straight in front of you at the start, not in a wiggly pile of slack—and not too long, say twenty-five feet or so.

In the normal grip of a fly rod, the reel hangs down from the wrist vertically.

For the side cast, turn the wrist 90 degrees, knuckles facing down and reel horizontal.

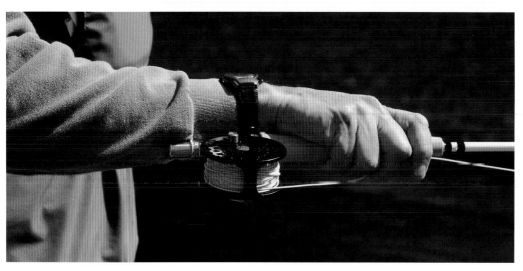

When making a backhanded side cast, the wrist still turns 90 degrees, but the knuckles remain facing up. The rod guides still face the front.

Unlike an overhead cast, it is usually easier to make this cast standing side on to the target. For a right-handed caster, keep the left shoulder facing the front, and vice versa for a left-handed, or back-handed, caster. This makes it much easier to track the low back and forward loops, ensuring they stay out of trouble.

Your stance should be sideways to the target with your left foot forward for a right-handed cast.

With a left-handed, or backhanded, cast the right foot needs to be forward.

Like all to-and-fro casts, you are trying to form a nice tight loop, retaining good line speed. This is achieved by keeping the rod tip traveling in a straight line path and having a smooth acceleration to a positive stop on both the back and forward cast.

The essential difference between this cast and the regular overhead cast is the fact that the line (and rod) travels on a horizontal plane. This means that your loop may only be traveling two feet or so above the water during the entire cast. Your casting stroke needs to be pretty fast; otherwise your loop will drop and touch the water. You can make this cast with your rod tip only a foot above the water and keep a really low loop, or as much as four feet above the water—still on a horizontal plane—and have more height and time to make the cast. It just depends on why you are making this cast.

The longer the line you carry outside the rod, or the lower you want your loop to travel, the faster your casting stroke has to be.

To get a loop as close to the water as possible (to get under low branches or obstructions), you may need to crouch down and lower your shoulder height. This will lower your arm height, which in turn lowers your rod tip and loop.

For a normal side cast, the rod tip (and thus the fly line) travels about waist height.

To get a really low loop, drop the rod tip close to the water. This is easiest to do when crouching low. Remember to make sure the rod tip travels at a high speed to keep a low traveling line like this from hitting the water.

You can cheat a bit with this cast to help things along. If you have an obstruction in front of you and need a low front loop to get underneath, tilt the plane of your casting stroke slightly. Still keep the rod tip traveling on a horizontal plane, but have the backcast rising about 15 degrees above the horizontal and the forward cast about 15 degrees below. This does two things. First, it gives you a higher backcast and a little more time to get the cast right. More important, the slightly rising backcast automatically makes the forward cast fire lower and slightly downwards.

If the obstructions are behind you, then just reverse this concept and have the forward cast rising, helping the backcast stay low.

This cheat is fine if the reason you are making the side cast is to keep your fly under an obstruction, but does not work so well for the gentle presentation or for bending the line around an obstacle. For the best result in these requirements, keep your planes totally flat and parallel to the water.

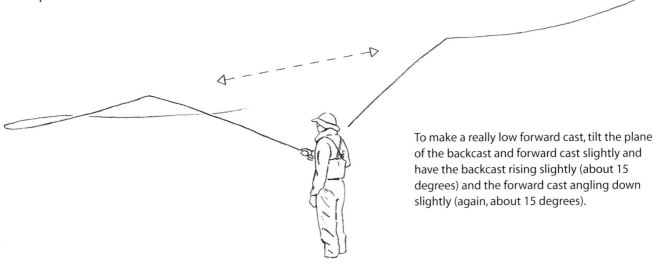

To make a really low forward cast, tilt the plane of the backcast and forward cast slightly and have the backcast rising slightly (about 15 degrees) and the forward cast angling down slightly (again, about 15 degrees).

Presentation

When you make a regular overhead cast and have the two legs of the loop traveling in a vertical plane, it is hard to achieve the very softest in presentation. If you have slightly too much speed, the line accelerates and kicks over faster than desired. Even if you get it right and your loop unrolls five feet above the water, then it has five feet to drop.

With the side cast, if you have too much acceleration, the line will still land feather soft (though it might kick and land off target), and it should only have one to two feet to drop to the water—both great factors in providing a nice, light presentation.

However, what I really like about the side cast is that the whole forward cast comes into position from a low plane. Even with a perfect overhead cast the forward loop comes in from a great height, making it far more visible and obvious to spooky fish in clear, calm waters. With the side cast, the line sneaks in nice and low.

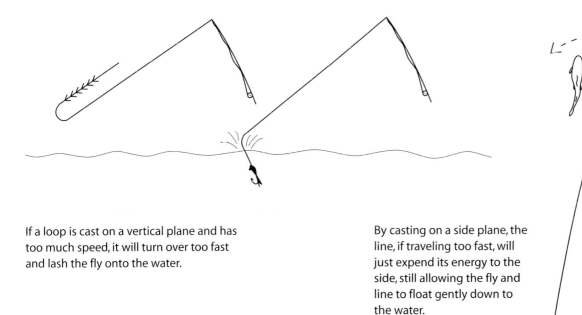

If a loop is cast on a vertical plane and has too much speed, it will turn over too fast and lash the fly onto the water.

By casting on a side plane, the line, if traveling too fast, will just expend its energy to the side, still allowing the fly and line to float gently down to the water.

Viewed from a low position like this, the side cast has very little time in the fish's window and sneaks a fly into position.

With a regular overhead cast, the line is much more visible and can spook wary fish.

A master at this sneaky cast is Jerry Siem, the phenomenally talented rod designer at Sage. He uses this sneaky side plane in all walks of fly fishing, from spring creeks to bonefish flats to permit and tarpon. Anywhere he needs a low, unobtrusive presentation, he turns his loop on the side. Jerry's trick, however, is to do this with the rod in a vertical plane. That is awesome and takes tremendous control, but then he is a tremendous caster! The advantage Jerry's technique has is that you can cast much longer lengths of line with your rod in a vertical plane than you can with your rod tip a foot above the water.

It is a tricky casting technique to master. The buildup to the final presentation cast is a regular overhead cast (forearm vertical, keeping the rod in a vertical plane, and wrist cocking and uncocking on the same vertical plane), but the final front loop is turned on its side by a fast rotation of the wrist—turning the knuckles of the casting hand from facing out and to the side to suddenly facing toward the target at the last instance. At the same time, Jerry thrusts his hand up about six inches. This has the effect of dropping the fly below the standing line and aiding the sneaky approach. It takes very precise timing and a great deal of practice to master this, but it is worth the effort!

Jerry fishes this technique using a leader with a level tippet that is longer than normal, about four feet. This allows the fly to land softly, but also with some slack so that it sinks immediately.

I like this technique for the under-the-radar approach of a fly, but for general side cast conditions—keeping your fly line under an obstacle, or bending the line around an object—the standard side cast I described earlier is certainly easier to master.

Jerry Siem's long-range version of the side cast has the rod traveling in a vertical plane, making a regular overhead cast, with the wrist in a vertical plane until and including the final backcast.

The final forward cast starts the same way as a normal overhead cast.

At the moment of power, when the wrist usually turns the rod over and stops, Jerry twists his wrist 90 degrees in the cast, turning the loop to a horizontal plane.

Fault Finding

Unlike the continuous motion casts, the side cast has few mistakes, and they are relatively easy to cure. Nevertheless, here's a few to look out for.

1 **The backcast (or the forward cast) keeps hitting the water.** The line may be too long for such a cast, you have too long a pause between each casting stroke, or the casting plane isn't horizontal. Remember to keep the fly line short, the casting stroke fast, and the rod on a horizontal plane.

You don't want the fly to hit the water during the side cast. If it does, speed up the casting stroke slightly and make sure the rod tip is traveling on a horizontal plane.

2 **The fly keeps getting caught in the obstruction you are trying to get under.** The rod was not traveling horizontally enough, or was horizontal but too high. Crouch low to drop your rod tip to a lower position and tilt the cast slightly so that the one heading toward the obstruction travels 15 degrees below the horizontal and the opposite cast travels 15 degrees above.

If you keep snagging the obstacle you are trying to get under, try crouching down and lowering your rod height. Also try raising the backcast so that it helps fire the forward cast low.

3 **The fly does not land where it was aimed.** The side cast is a tough cast to get accurate because you cannot track a straight and vertical rod path. It just takes practice, but make sure your rod is traveling a straight path to the target and you judge the speed of the cast so that there is just enough speed for the loop to unroll. Too fast a cast will make the loop kick as it unravels and flick the fly to the side.

Making an accurate cast with the side cast is tougher than with an overhead cast. Plenty of practice is required, but make sure you practice with the rod tip traveling in a straight line to the target, and judge the line speed to have just enough power to unroll; otherwise, with too much power, it will lash out of plane and kick the fly to the side of where you are aiming.

CHAPTER 15

The Shepherd's Crook Cast

To-and-Fro Group

The shepherd's crook cast is one of the most useful river casts there is. What I like about it is the fact that it is a very satisfying cast to perform. As you will have probably gathered, I am a caster and really enjoy casting for the sake of casting, so any cast that is particularly challenging works for me!

In the United States, the shepherd's crook is called the positive curve cast or the negative curve cast, depending on what you do with the line. I'll discuss that shortly.

There are many reasons you might want to bend the end of your fly line 90 degrees. Here's a few that I use this cast for.

1. Fishing directly upstream to a fish that I would line if casting straight to it.
2. Casting a fly around a rock, patch of weed, or bridge abutment.
3. Casting into a cut, or bay, in the bank that I am standing on.

When to use this cast: Any situation that requires bending the front end of the fly line 90 degrees or so.

In this fishing situation, with a fish directly upstream of me, a straight cast that lands the fly upstream of the fish will mean casting my leader over its head and, most likely, spooking it.

Instead, by casting the line to one side and then bending the line around in a curve, I can make the cast and not spook the fish.

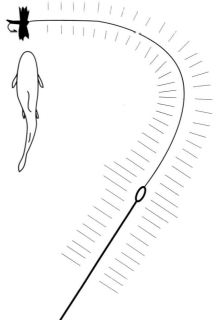

135

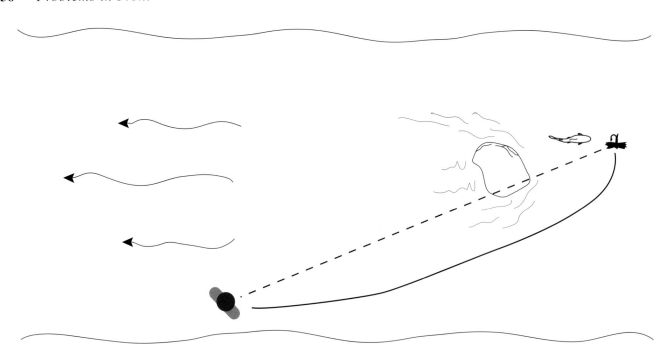

Another situation that is perfect for the shepherd's crook cast is when confronted with an obstacle in between you and the target. Here, a straight cast to the fish will land the line on top of the boulder and probably snag it. By aiming to the right-hand side and then bending the line tip to the left, one can still land the fly in the right place and avoid any danger of snagging the obstacle.

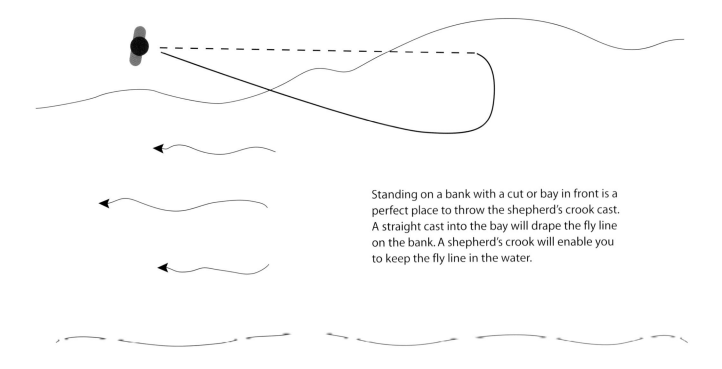

Standing on a bank with a cut or bay in front is a perfect place to throw the shepherd's crook cast. A straight cast into the bay will drape the fly line on the bank. A shepherd's crook will enable you to keep the fly line in the water.

The first and most important thing to know about this cast is the correct leader rig. In order to bend the fly line 90 degrees, the loop must have high line speed and, more important, it must turn over with speed. You cannot get a fast turnover with a long, fine, delicate leader. The best leader for this type of cast has plenty of butt section, a good steep taper, and is relatively short. It's hard to quantify what short is as this depends on rod length and line weight and, to some extent, fly size. As a guideline, I would work with a 7-foot leader with maybe 4 feet of level butt section, a 2-foot section that is tapered, and only 1 foot of level tip. At least this will make the cast as easy as possible, yet retain a leader design that will still fish nicely. (The perfect leader to cast with would have 4 feet of level butt material, say 30-pound mono, period! But that wouldn't fish too well!)

If you remember in the previous chapter, I mentioned that one of the uses of the side cast was to bend your line around an object. If you have a good side cast in your repertoire, you are halfway there. If you have a good side cast and the right leader design, you are 80 percent there. The remaining 20 percent is what you do to make the line bend. This is achieved by reversing the direction of the loop's momentum.

So to make the line kick, you need to reverse the direction of the lower leg of the loop. You can do this by giving the fly line a short tug with your free hand as the line is unrolling, or you can do it by twitching the rod tip back. Either method works and both result in a beautiful curve in the line. Remember that this cast comes from a side cast. If you reverse the loop direction of an overhead cast, the line will kick in a vertical plane and smash into the water.

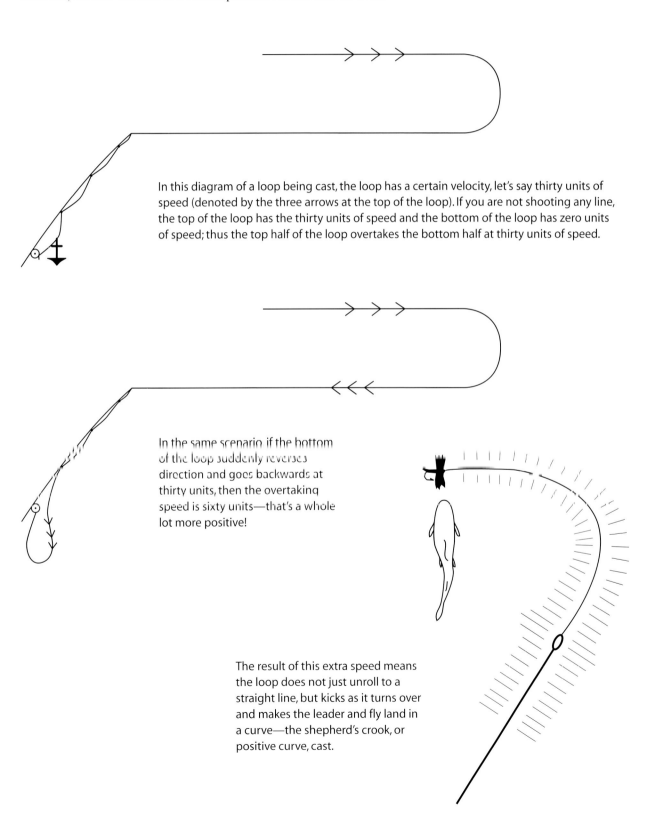

In this diagram of a loop being cast, the loop has a certain velocity, let's say thirty units of speed (denoted by the three arrows at the top of the loop). If you are not shooting any line, the top of the loop has the thirty units of speed and the bottom of the loop has zero units of speed; thus the top half of the loop overtakes the bottom half at thirty units of speed.

In the same scenario, if the bottom of the loop suddenly reverses direction and goes backwards at thirty units, then the overtaking speed is sixty units—that's a whole lot more positive!

The result of this extra speed means the loop does not just unroll to a straight line, but kicks as it turns over and makes the leader and fly land in a curve—the shepherd's crook, or positive curve, cast.

The easiest way to make a shepherd's crook cast (while making a side cast) is to hold the line in your left hand (assuming you are a right-handed caster) and keep your left hand close to the rod and right hand during the cast.

As you make the final forward cast, give a short, sharp tug of the line with your left hand.

This has the effect of reversing the direction of the bottom half of the loop and making the front end of the loop kick into the shepherd's crook shape. In this picture, you can see the splash made by the fly and how much it is to the side of the fly line. This is the object of the shepherd's crook cast.

One of the hardest things with this cast is the aim. Do not aim at where you want the fly to land; instead, aim your cast where you want the fly *line* to land, bending the fly line tip, leader, and fly away from this point. A lot of people look directly at the fish and then make the cast, aiming at the fish. All this will do is land the fly line on the fish and bend the fly away from it.

Making the curve is easy; controlling it is a little harder. With the right leader, a good side cast, and only a tiny amount of practice, you will be able to bend the fly line in no time. Now comes the tough bit—bending it the amount you want to. In theory this is easy. If your loop is unrolling and you have, say, 10 feet of loop that has not yet unrolled and you tug, you will kick that amount of line round to the side. In other words, if you want to bend the line 10 feet, tug when there is 10 feet of loop left; if you want 3 feet of bend, tug when there is only 3 feet to unroll.

Practice is, as ever, important for mastering this cast, and I remember practicing this cast on the local playing fields when I was growing up. I jammed a stick in the ground and then laid my hat to one side and behind. I walked back 20 feet or so and then aimed my fly line to the left of the stick and tried to bend the fly line and land the fly on my hat. I varied the distance the hat was to the side of the stick to practice big bends and little bends, and also switched the hat to the other side of the stick to get the line to bend the other direction.

If you don't have water nearby to practice this cast, go to the local playing field. I used to jam a stick (or a cricket stump) into the ground about twenty-five feet from me and then lay my hat on the ground behind the stick and to one side. I would practice bending my line around the stick and try to land it on the hat.

The theory, as I say, is easy. Just bear one thing in mind: the bigger the bend or curve you want in the line, the faster your line speed needs to be and the faster you have to make the line kick. This means having a greater overtaking speed between the top leg and the bottom leg. I would say you would need more like fifty units of speed on the top leg and fifty units of speed on the bottom leg to throw a big bend in the line, so make a faster cast with a more aggressive tug. Conversely, for a small amount of bend you don't want a high line speed. Slow your casting stroke down and shorten and soften the tug.

By varying the hat's position, you can practice many different scenarios. Here I have thrown a large bend into the line. I have done this by accelerating my forward cast (as well as tightening my loop) and giving a good hard tug with my left hand.

For a smaller amount of bend, like in this photo, you don't need so much line speed or such an aggressive tug.

If you are a right-handed caster, you will always throw a curve, or bend, to the left. That is just the nature of the loop's momentum from a side cast. As a left-handed caster, you will always bend or curve the line to the right. Sometimes you need to bend the line the other way, so how do you do that? Well, you just read the answer—you just change hands. Either that or make a backhanded side cast. Both directions are useful, as you never know which way you are going to have to bend the fly line.

Every caster should also have the ability to bend the line to the right. This is either achieved by making the cast with the left hand, or if this feels weak and uncontrollable, use the right hand and cast from the backhand side.

There is one other way to make your fly line land in a curve, and that is to collapse the loop. If you make a right-handed side cast and accelerate the line, it will kick to the left. However, if you were to make the loop collapse you would land the fly to the right. Do this by feeding slack at exactly the moment you want the line to collapse. Instead of starting the side cast with your hands close together, start with them about three feet apart. Make the side cast as usual, and before the loop has unrolled, suddenly push your two hands together. This sudden rush of slack line up the guides will make the loop's turnover collapse and give you a curved line to the right-hand side.

There are reasons to practice both. Let's say you need to bend the line to the right but have obstructions on the left side of your body that make it impossible to make a backhanded or left-handed side cast. This collapsed loop version will ensure you get the job done!

Many anglers call this cast either the positive curve cast or the negative curve cast, and there is some debate as to which is a positive curve and which is a negative curve. If you bend the line to the left, is that positive or negative? To me the answer is simple: If your cast is achieved by accelerating the turnover, that is a positive curve. If you collapse the turnover and take all the line speed out, that is a negative curve cast, regardless of which hand you cast with.

To make a side cast collapse into a shepherd's crook, start with your two hands about three feet apart, your left hand (for the right-handed caster) holding the fly line, and maintain this gap throughout the entire backstroke and part of the forward stroke.

At the point you want the line to collapse on the forward stroke, quickly give the cast some slack from your left hand toward the rod.

This will make the loop drop onto the water without turnover but with a curve to the caster's right.

Fault Finding

1 **"I can't get the line to kick at all."** You need a high line speed to get the line to kick around in a curve, and usually if there is no kick, it is because you don't have enough line speed to get the line to kick around. This could be because the leader design is wrong, so check this first. If the leader is right, your loops might be too big or your rod and casting stroke are just not generating enough line speed.

2 **"I can't land the fly where I want to."** If you are managing to bend the leader and fly line but cannot control where you land the fly, you have mistimed the tug. If your fly shoots too far past the target, you have tugged too early and got a large bend in the line. If you are falling short of the target, you have tugged too late and don't have enough bend in the line to take the fly to the target.

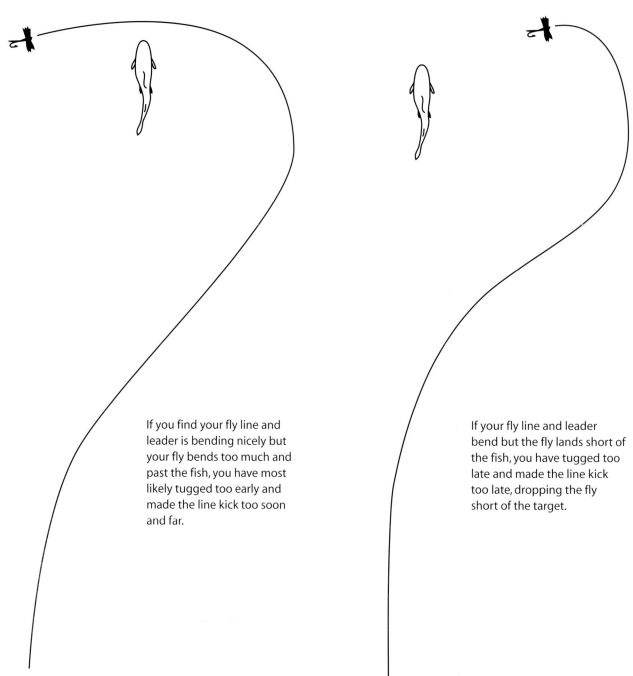

If you find your fly line and leader is bending nicely but your fly bends too much and past the fish, you have most likely tugged too early and made the line kick too soon and far.

If your fly line and leader bend but the fly lands short of the fish, you have tugged too late and made the line kick too late, dropping the fly short of the target.

3 **"I keep landing the fly line on the fish and bending the fly away from it."** This is just an aiming issue. Remember to aim and look at where you want the fly line to land on the water and not where you want the fly to kick to.

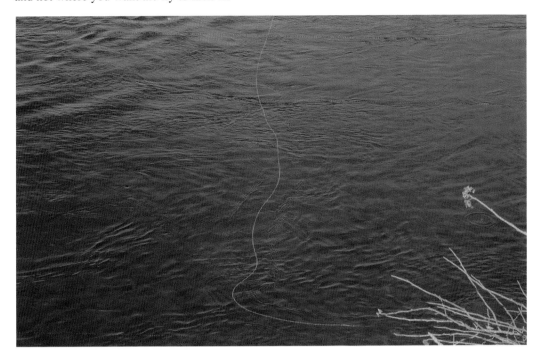

If you make a cast and find your fly line lands in a straight line toward the target and then bends the fly away from it, you have aimed at the wrong spot. In this photo, I have aimed directly at the camera and then tugged. This has placed the fly line tip, leader, and fly out of the picture.

To get the actual fly (circled) to land in line with the camera, I had to aim my line several feet to the side, as you can see. However, if you look at the splash caused by the fly, you will see that I have achieved my goal.

CHAPTER 16

The Reach Cast

To-and-Fro Group

The reach cast is an excellent cast for the river fly fisher—particularly those wading close to the bank or standing on the bank and fishing directly upstream or downstream. Unlike the shepherd's crook cast, the reach cast is designed to move the back end of the fly line, the part nearest the rod, not the front end as the shepherd's crook cast does. It might sound tricky, but luckily, it is ridiculously easy to do!

The main reason for moving the rear end of the fly line is to move it out of the way of an obstacle close to you. Let's say you are wading a creek, fishing upstream, and a large boulder is in front of you. You need to make a cast twenty feet or so up-

> **When to use this cast:** Any situation that requires moving the fly line nearest the rod to a different position.

stream, but if you make a straight cast, you will land your line on top of the boulder. The boulder is too close to you to use a shepherd's crook cast, so you use a reach cast.

Unlike the shepherd's crook cast, with the reach cast you actually aim where you want your fly to land. Make a regular overhead cast toward the target, and then finish with a normal forward cast. However, before your fly line lands, you want to move your rod and casting arm smoothly to one side. The amount of movement depends on how much you want to move the rear end of the line. Here are a few photos that illustrate how to make this cast.

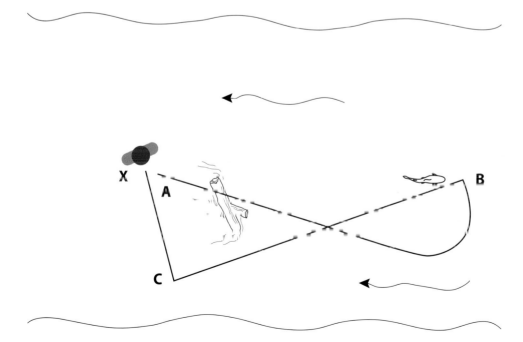

In this fishing situation, with a fish directly upstream of the angler (at A) and a boulder or log close in front, a shepherd's crook cast will not work. This is where the reach cast is so successful. The reach cast effectively changes the position of where you are standing, in this example to C.

Another situation where a reach cast is particularly useful is when standing on (or close to) a riverbank and casting the fly to a bankfeeder, tight in. A straight line cast in this situation will probably result in landing the fly line on the bank and snagging it on the grass.

Start the reach cast with a regular overhead cast, making sure you have a loop of slack held in your noncasting hand.

Aim the cast at where you want the fly to land.

Just as you complete the final forward cast, and before your front loop has unrolled, let the slack line go from your line hand.

While the loop is in the air and traveling toward the target, smoothly slide your rod to the side about 90 degrees, making sure the slack line you have is pulled up through the rod rings by moving the rod to the side, not by shooting line on the cast.

Keep holding the rod to the side as the fly line falls toward the water.

Watch the fly land on target and the fly line fall to the side and clear of the obstacles.

You need the loop of slack to make sure your cast lands where you aimed it. If you don't have the loop of slack and complete the reach cast, you will pull the fly back toward you and short of the target.

This cast has a couple of important factors. The first is that you must have some slack line ready to shoot. Do not shoot this slack line as part of the forward casting stroke. Instead let the front loop get to the point where it has almost unrolled, and then let go of the slack. You need to let the slack go just as you move the rod tip to the side and use the sideways movement of the rod to take out the slack line. This slack allows the fly to land where you aimed it, without being pulled off course by the sideways movement of the rod. You must complete the sideways rod movement and shoot slack before the fly line lands.

The amount of slack depends on how much you move your rod tip to the side. In the most extreme case, you might move your rod 90 degrees to the side. A 9-foot-long rod and a 2-foot-long arm makes a pull of 11 feet. You will need to shoot 11 feet of slack to ensure the fly does not get pulled back.

To state the obvious, the direction you move the rod influences the direction you move the fly line. If you have an obstacle in front and need to reach your line to the right, then move your rod to the right. If you want to move the line to the left, move the rod to the left. You don't need to change hands or reverse the direction of the cast to get the line to move a different way.

Fault Finding

1 **"When I make my reach move I keep moving the fly and pulling it short of the target."**
Simply, you have either not shot enough slack line, or you have let the slack line go at the wrong moment. If either of those are the case, when you move the rod to the side you will pull the fly back. To avoid this, you need to let the slack go in your noncasting hand as you move the rod to the side. Too early a release of slack or too late and all you will do is pull the fly back toward you.

If you find you are pulling the fly backwards and landing it short of the target, you are not feeding enough slack line to compensate for the sideways rod movement. Or you may have moved you rod first and then let the slack go.

Make sure you have slack in your hand and ready to feed and let go before you move the rod to the side. Also make sure you have enough slack to allow for the distance the rod tip will travel sideways.

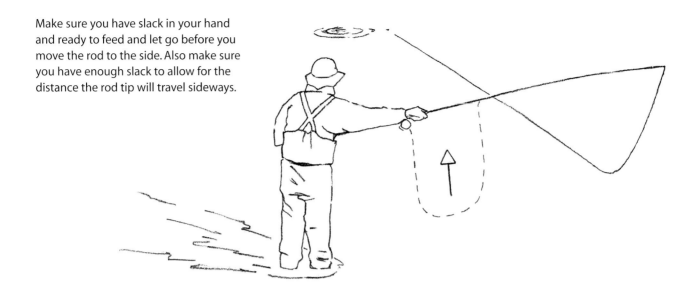

2 **"When I move my rod, I throw a curve or mend in the line."** A true reach cast lands in a straight line. All you should be doing is moving the point where that line starts. You could do the same thing by moving yourself to a new point, but sometimes you just can't or don't want to do that. If you get a curve in the line, it is most likely because you have actually moved your rod to the side and then back to where it started. When you make a reach cast and have moved the rod to the side to steer the line around an obstacle, leave the rod to the side and fish the line with the rod tip there.

Make sure you leave your rod pointing to the side when the reach has finished, and fish the fly from that position.

CHAPTER 17

The Aerial Mend

To-and-Fro Group

Let me start by explaining what a mend is. A mend is a river fly fisher's cast that repositions the fly line to allow the fly to fish more naturally. Most people who use a mend do so by putting the mend into the line after the fly line has landed and the fly has started to fish. There are times when you want a mend much quicker than this and when you want the line to land already with a mend, and the aerial mend is perfect for these situations.

A regular mend is made once the fly line has landed, so why the aerial mend?

1. If you are fishing a sinking line, you will need an aerial mend. It is impossible to throw a mend into the fly line once it has landed on the water and the line has sunk.

2. Sometimes you cast your fly into a backeddy, or a current that has vastly different speeds between where your fly lands and where the majority of your fly line lands. In this situation, any delay at all between the fly landing and the mend means your fly will immediately start to fish unnaturally.

3. Sometimes you need to throw your mend right by the tip of the fly line. A regular mend at any distance cannot be thrown far from where you stand.

Like the reach cast, this cast is performed with a regular overhead cast. No need to change hands for different directions and no need to have high line speed to kick the curve into the

When to use this cast: Any situation that requires putting a mend in the line, but particularly when the mend has to be instantaneous.

fly line. Instead, you need just an easy, smooth movement of the rod tip from left to right (or from right to left, depending on whether you want the mend to land with a curve to the left of the line or a curve to the right of the line). Again, shooting slack is an integral part of this cast. If you don't, just like the reach cast, you will pull your fly toward you and short of the target.

To make an aerial mend, just make your regular overhead cast, but have a few feet of slack held in your noncasting hand. Aim your fly at where you want it to land. After the rod has stopped moving, but before any part of the line has touched the water, let the slack go and move your rod tip about five feet to one side and immediately back to the original position. Both the side movement and the back movement should occur before the fly line lands on the water and before all the slack in the line has pulled out.

The aerial mend is easy to do, but just like the shepherd's crook cast, it takes some practice to throw the right size mend that you want, as well as position it exactly where you want.

The size of the mend is controlled by how much you move the rod tip to the side. If you move your rod tip only two to three feet to the side (and back again), you will get a relatively small mend, or curve, in the line. If you move your rod tip eight or nine feet to the side, you will get a big mend.

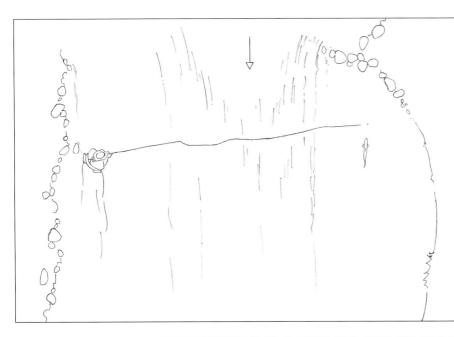

Imagine you are fishing a river with a fast current in the middle and a fish is lying in slower water on the far side. You want to cast your fly to this fish.

If you make an ordinary cast, and do nothing, the faster current will bow your line into a curve and drag the fly faster than the water that the fish is lying in. This is pretty unnatural and usually ignored by any self-respecting fish.

The solution is to throw a curve in the line that is the opposite of the curve that the current will make. This curve is called a mend. The mend allows your fly to sit in the slower water for a period of time while the faster current collapses your mend, creating slack. You will get a few seconds of precious fishing time as your fly moves in the slow water at the correct speed before your slack line washes straight and the current drags the fly out too fast. This is the value of a mend.

An aerial mend is a way to throw a mend in your fly line in midair. The line will land with a mend so that the fly can fish correctly immediately.

Make a small aerial mend by only moving the rod tip a couple of feet to the side and back again while the line is in the air.

Make a large aerial mend by making a much bigger movement of the rod tip, say eight to nine feet.

Harder than controlling the size of the mend is controlling the position of it. You never know what situation you will come across when fishing a river. Sometimes you are going to need to throw a mend in the line that is right at the tip of the fly line, close to the leader. Sometimes you will need the mend closer to you than that, and sometimes you will even need the mend to be right under your rod tip. It just depends on where the influencing current is.

A good exercise is to practice on grass and jam three sticks in the ground—one fifteen feet from where you are standing, one at twenty-five feet, and one at thirty-five feet. Practice casting and mending your line around each stick. Aim your fly line to the left of the sticks, but try to make a mend around only one of them. Once you have mastered the near stick, move to the middle stick and then to the far stick. Once you can achieve a mend to the right around each stick, try to make a mend to the left, casting your fly line to the right of all sticks and throwing your mend around the chosen one.

Positioning the mend requires timing. There is an amount of time between when your rod tip stops moving at the end of the forward cast and when your line lands on the water—for the sake of simplicity let's say it is three seconds. To get a mend close to you and around the near stick, wait two seconds after the rod tip has stopped before making the side-to-side movement of the rod tip. For the middle stick, wait only one second, and for the far stick, don't wait at all. In the case of the farthest stick, the mend should start immediately as the rod comes to a stop. The quicker you can move your rod side to side to create the mend, the farther it is away from you.

Practice around sticks like these to get confident and competent at throwing a mend where you want and as big, or as small, as you want so you will be ready for anything you come across on a river.

A good exercise is to place three sticks in the ground, one fifteen feet from where you are standing, one twenty-five feet, and one thirty-five feet.

Practice casting and throwing mends around each stick in turn. A mend to the right requires landing all the fly line, the leader, and the fly to the left of the sticks, but mending the line around the right of one. Here I have made a mend around the close stick. To do this, you wait until the rod tip has finished the final forward cast and almost all the fly line has landed, and then move your rod right and then left, shooting slack at the same time.

Here the mend is around the middle stick. Do this by having only a slight pause between when the rod stops at the end of the forward cast and moving side to side to create the mend.

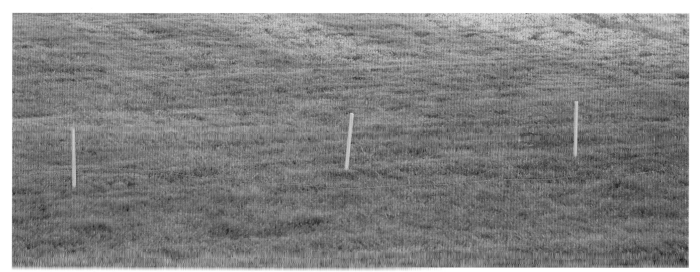

To get the mend as far away from you as possible (and around the third stick) you need to have high line speed and a very, very curly mend. There should be absolutely no pause between when the rod has stopped on the final forward cast and the mend movements. Again, shooting slack as you mend is vital to prevent pulling the fly back toward you.

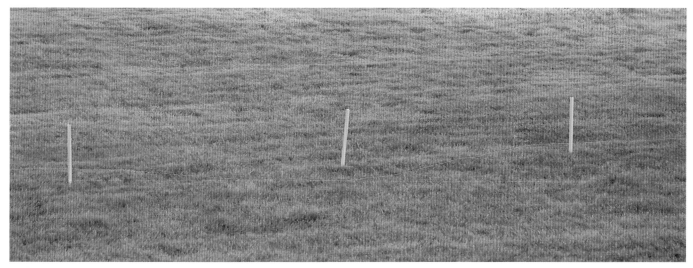

With such grass practice, don't forget there will be many times when fishing that you will actually need to throw a mend in the other direction. All the above photos show the mend to the right and the line curving to the right around the stick. Also practice throwing mends to the left around each stick, as in this mend around the middle stick.

Fault Finding

1 **"When I make my aerial mend I move the fly towards me."** Just as with the reach cast, you must let slack go before you make any additional movements of the rod. The slack you are releasing, not the line that is in the air, will form the mend. If you are releasing slack and still pulling the fly backwards, either you have released too late to affect the mend, or you did not have enough slack.

Make sure you have some slack in your free hand and are ready to feed, and be ready to let go before you move the rod to the side. Also, make sure you have enough slack to allow for the distance the rod tip will travel sideways. Here I am holding the fly line tight as I make my mend. This is a common problem and will cause the fly to land well short of the fish.

2 **"I can't put the mend where I want it."** You are mistiming the sideways rod movement. If your mend is closer than you want, you have moved your rod side to side too late. If your mend is farther away than you want, you have moved your rod too early.

CHAPTER 18

Slack-Line Casts

To-and-Fro Group

A s a casting instructor and addicted caster, it sometimes seems a little strange to tell people that "a straight cast is no good," but indeed, many times you want your line to land in a bit of a pile of knitting—swinging a wet fly across a current for steelhead or salmon, for example. If you make a die-straight cast in this situation, your fly will start to swing immediately, not giving it time to sink and get to a good fishing depth. Better (for catching fish, anyway) is a cast that lands with some slack, allowing your fly to sink and fish at a decent depth and speed.

There are many other times when you need slack, and I'll mention a few examples in this chapter. However, the first thing to know is how to throw slack in the line.

> **When to use this cast:** Any situation that requires putting a pile of slack in the line.

There are a number of options depending on what you want to achieve. In the previous situation (swinging wet flies for salmon or steelhead), I would probably throw in an aerial mend. Another way is to design a long, level, and light leader that will not turn over with any authority and, thus, land with slack. If I was fishing for a selective trout on Henry's Fork, I might apply this method, using an 18-foot leader or so, based on a tapered 9-foot, 5X leader, but adding 9 feet of level 5X or 6X as tippet. Almost every cast made with a rig like this will land with slack! If you want slack on every cast, then this is a good way to achieve that.

If you want something a little more controlled, so you can put slack in when you need to, not on every cast, there are a number of options.

Big Loop

Good casters can control the size of their casting loops, both back and front. If you need slack, one way to add it is to open up the front loop of the final cast and make it more rounded. This will slow down the speed of the turnover and usually result in slack. (It depends on just how big you make your loop.)

Any cast you make that you want to land with some slack has to have a slower line speed, and probably a wider loop, than a normal cast. Even long leaders will turn over if there is enough line speed.

Outside the two methods I just mentioned (a long, fine leader and wide, open loop), and throwing a mend in the line (either regular or aerial), a few casting techniques can help. The main three are the side-to-side wiggle, the parachute cast, and loop control.

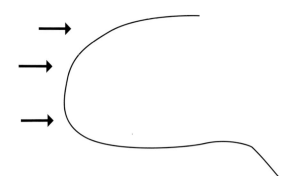

One way of making a fly line land with slack is to cast a very wide and rounded loop on the final presentation cast. A loop of these proportions has so much air resistance that it will not have any turnover speed and will usually fall with slack.

Almost the last thing you want when trying to cast slack is a tight loop. Whatever you do to create slack will be negated by the high line speed obtained from a small, tight, and efficient loop on the final cast.

Side-to-Side Wiggle

I don't know if that is exactly what it is called, but it is a pretty accurate name for it. When I learned this cast in England, it was called the slack-line cast, but after moving to the United States and finding other ways of throwing slack in the line, I had to give it another name.

If you have mastered the aerial mend and the reach cast, you will certainly have no problem mastering this cast. The essence of this cast, just like those other two, is the ability to let slack line go out of your free hand before the wiggle takes place.

What you are trying to do with this cast is to land your line in a series of S-shaped wiggles on the water. It's a pretty good way of getting a uniform amount of slack in the line.

The cast is easy enough. As you make your final forward cast, and before any fly line lands on the water, you move your rod tip to the right, then to the left, and then to the right again (and back to the left again, if you want more squiggles of slack). The rod tip should move on a horizontal plane, and the wiggles should not be fast or jerky, just smooth, with your rod deviating about four feet to the right of center then four feet to the left of center, and so on.

The more wiggles you get in before the fly line lands, the more S shapes you will have in the line. Likewise, the bigger the deviation of the rod tip from the center line (eight feet of move-ment instead of four feet), the bigger those S's will be.

As I mentioned at the start, what is imperative is the release of slack before you make the first squiggle and to have enough slack to last the amount of wiggles you do. If not, all the wig-gling you do with your rod tip will pull the fly back toward you—the line will land in a pile of S's, but the fly will not land where you intended.

The object of the side-to-side wiggle is to get your fly line to land with a fairly even series of S shapes, or squiggles, in the fly line.

If you want a large number of small squiggles in the line, move your rod tip side to side (only about two feet on either side of the center line), and make lots of fast rod tip wiggles.

For fewer squiggles, but with larger curves in the line, move your rod tip six to eight feet on either side of the center line and with only one or two rod tip wiggles. These should be slow and smooth.

Parachute Cast

This is one neat cast. I use this cast a lot, especially when fishing a dry fly downstream and trying to get a nice drag-free drift. You could use the side-to-side wiggle cast, but one of the downsides of this cast is that you land all your slack at the same time. If a fish took your fly immediately, you would have too much slack to have an effective hook set. The advantage of the parachute cast is that you control the slack you release. You give only enough slack for the fly to maintain a drag-free drift.

There are two slightly different ways of doing this cast. I'll start with the easiest one, the one where you can judge your fly's position most accurately.

Let's say a trout is rising downstream of you about thirty feet away. Start by positioning yourself so that the fish is not directly downstream of you but at more of a 45-degree angle. Make a regular overhead cast, but aim to land your fly a good five or six feet upstream of where the fish is feeding and a good seven or eight feet to the other side of the current line that leads directly to the fish. Let the fly and fly line land, but before any current has moved the fly, smoothly raise your rod tip and pull the fly across the current until it is directly upstream of the fish. Your rod should be almost pointing to the vertical at this stage. As soon as your fly is directly upstream of the fish, start to lower your rod tip back down toward the water. With a 9-foot rod, you can get about a 10-foot long drag-free drift, which is plenty to take your fly to the fish and beyond.

The key to this cast is to lower your rod at the same speed as the current is flowing. If you lower your rod slower than the current, you will hold back the fly and create drag. Lowering it faster than the current speed is the lesser of the two evils, as the only disadvantage is that you will have a little extra slack and make the hook set slightly slower than if you maintain the perfect rod tip drop.

To make a parachute cast, start by positioning yourself about 45 degrees upstream of a rising fish (Y). Make a regular overhead cast, and aim to land your fly a good five or six feet upstream of where the fish is lying and a good seven or eight feet to the other side of the fish, landing the fly at X.

As soon as the fly has landed and before the current has any effect on it, smoothly lift your rod tip toward a vertical position, dragging the fly back toward you until it is directly upstream of the fish.

As soon as your fly is upstream of the fish, start to lower your rod at the same speed as the current, giving slack to the fly and allowing it to drift downstream without any drag.

The other version of this cast is a little more difficult to control but has a distinct advantage. The other way is to do exactly the same thing as I have just described, but before the line and fly has landed, lift your rod and drag the fly into position. If you can get the fly directly upstream of the fish and with a high rod before anything has landed, you will avoid any chance of drowning the dry fly or spooking a fish. It is harder to be able to drag the fly into position with this method as you can't watch the dry fly skate its merry little way across the current and stop when the fly is in the right path, but it is another step in the evolution of the master caster.

Another way of making a parachute cast is to make the cast (aiming upstream and beyond the fish) as before, but lift the rod toward the vertical before the fly and line has landed. It takes a good eye and a fine touch to be able to pull the fly into the correct position before the line has landed, but the advantage is you won't drown the dry fly or spook a cautious fish—well worth the practice.

As with the other version, just lower your rod tip at the same speed as the current to maintain a successful drag-free drift.

Loop Control

With the other methods of creating slack I have just explained, you have very little chance of positioning slack in the leader. Usually the parachute cast, the side-to-side wiggle, and even the aerial mend put the slack in the main body of the line, which is fine in most situations. Occasionally, though, usually in a backeddy, you will need slack right in the leader.

When you land your fly in a current that is going a different way compared with the majority of the current between you and the fish, putting slack in the middle of the fly line will not aid this situation at all.

In such a situation, a cast with a heavily inclined forward cast and a wider loop than normal can solve the problem.

If you aim your forward cast up at an angle of 30 degrees or so, and couple that with a wider loop and a slower traveling line, you will always put slack in the leader. It is no good to only have an inclined forward cast. If you have high line speed and an inclined loop, the line speed will pull out most of the slack or make the line bounce back and put slack in the middle section again. You want both the higher trajectory and the slower line speed to get the leader to fall with slack.

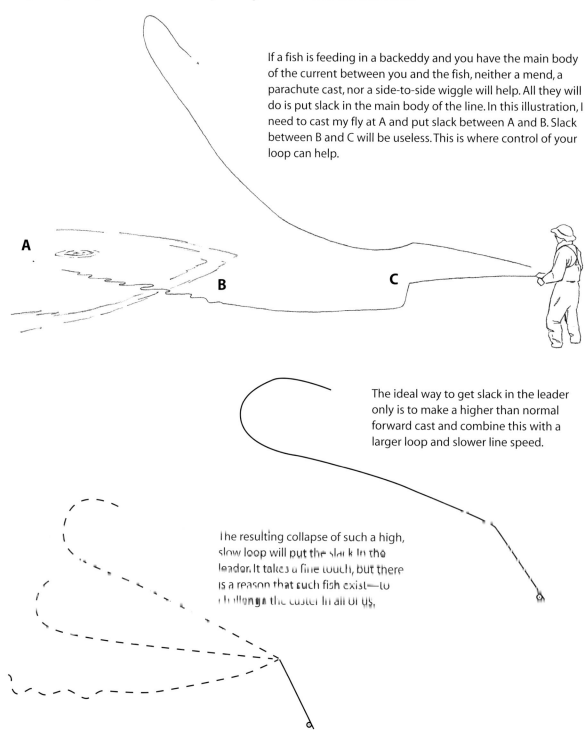

If a fish is feeding in a backeddy and you have the main body of the current between you and the fish, neither a mend, a parachute cast, nor a side-to-side wiggle will help. All they will do is put slack in the main body of the line. In this illustration, I need to cast my fly at A and put slack between A and B. Slack between B and C will be useless. This is where control of your loop can help.

The ideal way to get slack in the leader only is to make a higher than normal forward cast and combine this with a larger loop and slower line speed.

The resulting collapse of such a high, slow loop will put the slack in the leader. It takes a fine touch, but there is a reason that such fish exist—to challenge the caster in all of us.

COMBINED PROBLEMS

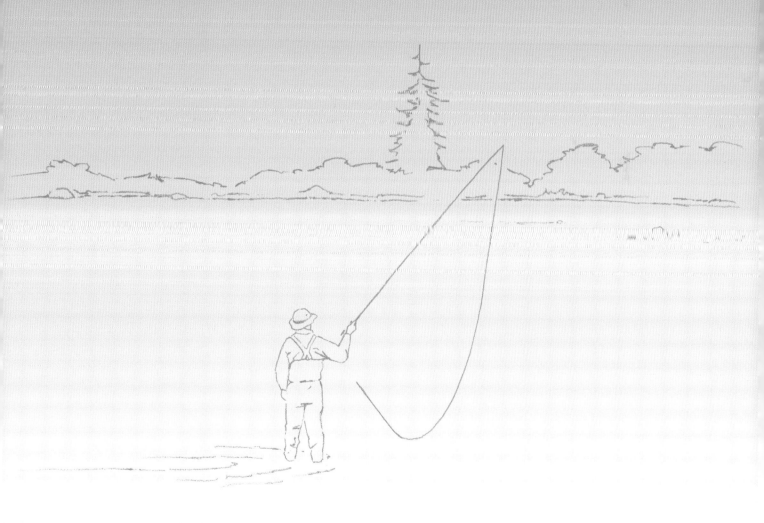

CHAPTER 19

The Roll Cast with Side Cut

I love casting and live for solving tricky fishing situations. I don't care if I catch a fish or not. If I can overcome a problem or two, get my fly to a fish, make it drift correctly, and then get the fish to take my fly, I am satisfied. What a day!

This section on combined problems deals with situations like the one I described above, ones that are a challenge to master but satisfying when you do. For those of you who see casting as just a way to catch a fish, this section will also help you catch fish—big fish, plenty of them, and ones that few other fly fishers can get their flies to.

Let's look at a problem and then think through the solution. Imagine you are fishing a small creek and you find a section where you are close to the bank with a few bushes behind you. The normal cast in this situation is a roll or spey cast.

Another situation is when you are fishing a similar small creek and a nice trout is rising under an overhanging branch in front of you. Here you would use a side cast to place your fly under the branch.

So when you come across a place where you have bushes behind you *and* an overhanging branch in front of you, what do

When to use this cast: Obstructions behind and an overhanging branch in front—no change of direction, short to mid-distance.

you do? A roll cast doesn't work because the forward cast unrolls vertically and will snag in the branch above the fish. A side cast is no good because the backcast will catch in the bushes behind. When you have both bushes behind you and an overhanging branch in front, you either step up to the plate and come up with something neat, or you go home!

The answer is to combine these two casts into a new cast—one that will solve both problems at the same time. Growing up in England and learning this cast from my dad, I learned that the solution was a cast called the roll cast with side cut. Lefty Kreh, in his excellent book *Casting with Lefty Kreh*, calls this the side roll. I like that name, but for the sake of good old English tradition (not to mention the fact that I have called it by another name for thirty years!), I will still refer to it as the roll cast with side cut.

Whatever you call it, you start this cast as you would a regular roll cast: by dragging your D-loop stroke back slowly, keeping the fly and line on the water, before lifting your rod to the key position. When you are in the key position, you wait for the D loop to sag behind your rod, creating enough load in the D loop to flex the rod,

The roll cast with side cut starts as a normal roll cast, with the rod in a vertical plane, angled back about 30 to 40 degrees, and a D loop hanging behind the rod.

If you look at your hand while in the key position, you will see that it starts in a vertical plane with your thumb on top and your knuckles pointing away from you and to the side.

Now for the forward stroke. Start the forward stroke with the rod in a vertical plane, but angled back to around 1 o'clock. It is imperative that you start with this high, vertical rod.

As your hand drives forward, you should roll it 90 degrees at the wrist from a vertical position with your thumb on top to a side position with your palm upwards. If you remember the ABC of the forward cast, this rotation must take place during the AB. As soon as your hand is in a horizontal position (and the rod too), you can accelerate this cast and finish with the BC—the power stroke.

You can enhance this wrist roll by lowering your shoulder and leaning to the side you are casting on.

Once your rod is on the horizontal plane, you need to power the cast, so finish off with a sharp acceleration, closing the wrist with a snap. This acceleration must remain on a horizontal plane to keep the loop on a horizontal plane and help it stay low and under the overhanging branch.

You cannot pause or hesitate between the start of the cast on the vertical plane and the finish of the cast, with the wrist snap, on the horizontal plane. It is like any other forward cast, accelerating smoothly from start to finish.

As your forward cast starts, your hand rolls over at the wrist until it is on a totally horizontal plane with your palm up. This wrist roll must take place while you are loading the rod—the AB of the forward cast.

This close-up shot of the hand shows that the wrist has rolled the hand into a horizontal plane.

Once the rod is horizontal, it should accelerate, staying on the horizontal plane and finishing with a nice, crisp wrist snap. The rod tip should travel on a horizontal plane from the start of the wrist roll until the stop of the casting stroke. Do not pause between the end of the wrist roll and the arm extension.

You need enough speed when you accelerate the rod to keep the fly line from dropping into the water. It is most vulnerable at this stage because the fly line is so close to the water.

The acceleration will impart enough speed in the line for it to break the tension of the water and lift into a perfect side cast.

If done correctly, the loop unrolls on a horizontal plane, low and close to the water.

There should be enough line speed so that the entire cast can unroll fully (and low) in the air before landing.

Because you have a low traveling loop, and because you have only a D loop to load the rod, not a full backcast, do not expect to make particularly long casts. With a 9-foot rod, I would say that 25 feet is about the maximum distance you could effectively make a roll cast with side cut.

Like all casts, practice this from both sides of your body, as you never know when you will have obstructions on one side of you that prevent you from making the cast you know.

One other use of this cast is a cheat. Many chapters ago, I described the rail track theory and how important it was not to cross the rail track. Well, this cast is a cheating way to get out of such problems. By turning your front loop on the side, it will avoid tangling the line if you cross the rail track. I use this cast in situations where I have positioned my rail track incorrectly and need to make a good forward cast, without starting the whole thing again.

With a regular roll cast, you have to obey the rail track law. Here, with my line at AB, I would need to make my forward cast somewhere to the right of the AB line. Aiming at EF will result in a tangle.

By rolling the rod to a horizontal plane and completing the roll cast with a side cut, I can still aim at EF and not get a tangle.

Fault Finding

This is not as easy a cast as it sounds or looks and many things can go wrong. Because the roll cast with side cut is a combination of two casts, it can have any of the problems from either the roll cast or the side cast as well as a few of its own! There is no point in going over the common roll cast mistakes again, nor the side cast ones, so let's look at the few issues that are unique to this cast.

1 **Tangling the line around the rod on the forward cast.** One of the critical things to avoid with this cast is making the forward cast and driving the rod into the D loop. Unfortunately, it is the most common mistake I see. When you start your forward cast, you must ensure that the rod and hand begin to travel forward before you roll your wrist and rod onto the horizontal plane. This ensures that the rod stays in front of the D loop throughout the forward cast. Do not cock the wrist back and drop the rod behind you to the horizontal plane before starting the forward cast. That puts the rod behind the D loop and guarantees that you wrap the line around the rod every time!

Make sure that the rod is well above the D loop while in the key position and stays above the D loop throughout the forward cast.

It is all too easy to cock the wrist back and hook the rod under the D loop before making the forward cast.

This will result in a tangle of the line around the rod every time.

2 **No power in the forward cast and a big slooshing sound, with loads of spray as the line leaves the water.** The easiest way to do this cast is to start with the rod laid back to a horizontal position (say 3 o'clock) and opposite the target, and just make a nice sideways forward stroke. Unfortunately, easy does not work here. If you start with your rod in a horizontal position, you will have the smallest D loop imaginable and a lot of line stuck on the water. That makes the slooshing sound you hear and the spray you see. If you allow the slightest hesitation, deceleration, or pause between when you turn your rod onto its side and the acceleration of the forward cast, the D loop will drop onto the water and ruin your day!

If you start with your rod in a horizontal position, you will have a tiny D loop and a huge amount of line drag. This cast will never work.

Start with your rod in a vertical plane and only move to the side plane as the forward cast accelerates into the final power stroke.

The perfect result!

CHAPTER 20

Spey Casts with Side Cut

When to use this cast: Obstructions behind and an overhanging branch in front—change of direction, mid-distance.

I want to start this chapter by introducing a new term: cast stringing. This is a term my dad came up with when we had our fly-fishing school in England. If it was a word in the Oxford English Dictionary, the dictionary entry might read:

cast stringing: the creation of a new fly cast from the components of established fly casts. The roll cast with side cut (the previous chapter) is a new cast made by combining the roll cast with a side cast. I guess you could also call these casts Frankenstein casts—new casts made from the bodies of other casts.

Actually, my dad (tongue in cheek . . . sort of) called them Heineken casts. At the time of the birth of these casts, the Heineken beer company had a series of ads on television in the UK that showed various beer drinkers unable to perform impossible tasks (like lifting a truck off a kid's bike). After a good slurp of Heineken, however, they could do it. The slogan was only Heineken can do this because it refreshes the parts other beers cannot reach. My dad paraphrased this with the cast stringing idea: only a Heineken cast can do this because it reaches the fish other casts cannot!

Whatever you call them, these series of casts have a very practical application, especially for the river fly fisher. You never know what situation you will come across when wading round the corner of a new river, so it is good to be prepared and be able to get your fly to the fish no matter what you find.

Apart from anything else, it is pretty cool to have an armory of assorted casts. Plain Jane might like popcorn-flavored Jelly Bellys, but it would be pretty dull eating that one flavor all the time.

In the previous chapter, I talked about the roll cast with side cut, which is the first of the Heineken casts. The main limitation with the roll cast with side cut is the lack of distance and the ability (or inability) to change direction when making the cast. It's great if your line is out there—somewhere in the direction of where you want your fly to go—but if you are fishing a river with a decent current and your line has swung round and ended up directly downstream of you, the roll cast with side cut is pretty ineffective.

As discussed earlier, with any of the continuous motion casts you have to have a rail track lined up with your target before you can make an effective forward stroke. This is where the spey cast with side cut comes in. It doesn't matter if you make a single spey or double spey, a snake roll or snap T, the principle is the same. The start of the cast is simply realizing, "Hey, it can be done."

The spey cast with side cut will also give you a lot more distance than the roll cast with side cut because you have an energetic and dynamic D loop. The rod will load deeper and will therefore spring with more speed, giving you more distance. This is just the next step in the evolution of you, the caster. Of course, this cast is harder to master than the aforementioned roll cast with side cut, but without challenges in your fly-casting life you may as well pick up a worm!

A roll cast starts with a small D loop; thus, distance will be limited. This applies equally to the roll cast with side cut.

Any of the spey casts (single spey, double spey, snake roll, or snap T) have a larger D loop behind the rod. This extra mass helps load the rod deeper and results in longer casts, assuming your timing is right! Again, the theory is relevant whether it is a regular spey cast or a spey cast with side cut.

So assuming you can make a normal spey, what next? What turns the spey cast you know into the spey cast with side cut?

The single spey with side cut starts as a normal single spey.

However, at the end of the D-loop stroke the rod tip must not rise to the 1 o'clock position but stay on a horizontal plane. The forward cast starts the instant the first piece of fly line (or leader) touches the water.

The forward stroke must have plenty of speed, and the rod tip must stay on a horizontal plane.

The loop and line will travel on a flat and low horizontal plane, avoiding the overhanging obstacles.

Just as with the roll cast with side cut, the difference between a normal single spey and a single spey with side cut is that the forward stroke is made on a horizontal plane instead of a vertical plane. There the similarity ends. With the roll cast with side cut, I stressed the importance of having the rod in a vertical plane when the D loop has formed. With any of the spey casts with side cut, you do not want this. You must make sure that the rod finishes the D-loop stroke in a horizontal plane. If the rod finishes in a vertical plane, your D loop will also be in a vertical plane. Even if you turn your rod onto the horizontal plane at the start of the forward stroke and make a sideways forward stroke, the D loop will remain in this vertical plane. Like any cast that tries to operate in two planes (a vertical D loop and a horizontal forward stroke), all you will end up with is a pile of crumpled line in front of you.

When making a spey cast with side cut (using whichever spey cast), do not finish the D-loop stroke with the rod raised in the vertical plane. The D loop will be in a vertical plane. When you make a forward stroke on a horizontal plane, the mismatch of the two planes will fire the forward cast into a great puddle a few feet in front of you.

Instead, you make the D-loop stroke stopping the rod on a horizontal plane, pointing 180 degrees from your intended target, and then make a regular side cast forward.

The only way to ensure that your forward cast does not take a nose dive into the water in front of you is to keep the rod in the horizontal plane when you have completed the D-loop stroke.

You must not drop your rod back to the horizontal plane—in other words, don't make a normal spey cast and then drop your rod down to the horizontal position. A dropping rod tip will only cause point P to go behind you and a lot of line to stick on the water, making it impossible to tear out.

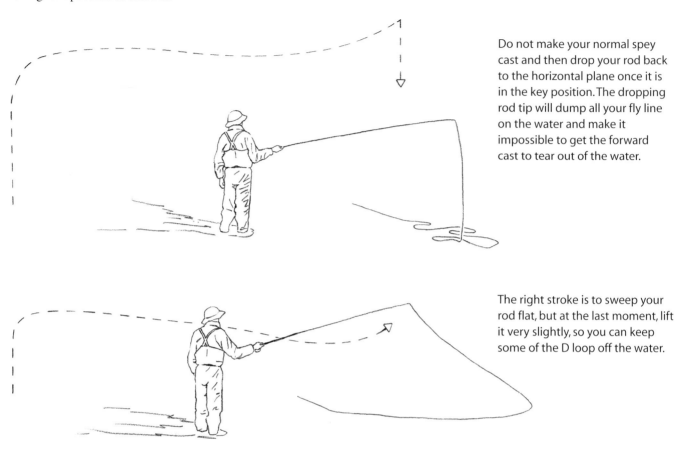

Do not make your normal spey cast and then drop your rod back to the horizontal plane once it is in the key position. The dropping rod tip will dump all your fly line on the water and make it impossible to get the forward cast to tear out of the water.

The right stroke is to sweep your rod flat, but at the last moment, lift it very slightly, so you can keep some of the D loop off the water.

You need to make the D-loop stroke with your rod traveling on a horizontal plane and stopping with your rod completely level and opposite your target. If you make the D-loop stroke with your rod on this plane, it will already be horizontal and level when you want to start the forward cast. No change of plane, no dropping rod tip, and no piles of knitting in front of you!

The only way to achieve the right forward stroke is for the rod to travel on a horizontal plane throughout the entire D-loop stroke. Thus, when you stop your rod at the key position, it is already horizontal.

One word of warning: you need a lot of speed in your D loop. Because your rod tip stops low and level (about four feet above the water) at the end of the D-loop stroke, you don't have any height to give you time for a slow D loop to form. Your D loop needs to be whizzing back so that it can completely form and have enough momentum to stay out of the water before you start the forward stroke. You also need to have perfect timing with the forward cast to avoid too much line falling into the water and getting stuck.

You need a fast-traveling D loop for the spey cast with side cut. It is imperative that the D loop has fully formed by the time you get the rod into the key position. This means you can start the forward cast right away—as soon as your rod reaches this horizontal key position.

Don't get this far and then ruin the cast with an ugly great mow of the rod tip forward, driving your rod through an arc. This will give you a large loop with no line speed that will fall in a miserable heap in front of you.

Fault Finding

Like the roll cast with side cut, this is a combination cast, so any faults could be because of the spey cast, the side cast, or something in the combination. Again, I won't go over the mistakes that might be caused by the base casts, but here's a couple of common ones that are unique to the spey cast with side cut.

1 **Too much line on the water at the start of the forward cast.** There are a bunch of possible causes of this! Timing is an obvious one. If you wait too long, you are going to get too much line stick. Assuming your timing is accurate, it is either because the D loop is traveling back too slowly and drops to the water before it has fully formed, or because the rod tip has come around on the D-loop stroke in more of a vertical plane and then dropped to the horizontal plane in preparation for the sideways forward cast.

A correctly timed forward cast will create a nice small anchor that leaves the water without a sound. Point P will still be in front of you.

If, when you start the forward cast, you hear a slurping noise and see lots of spray as the line tries to tear itself out of the water, you have too much line stick (line on the water behind you). The most likely causes of this are either that you have waited too long behind you before starting the forward stroke, or you have a slow, ineffective D-loop stroke, resulting in your D loop being formed before the rod gets into the key position.

2 **The forward cast tends to nose-dive into the water in front.** This is a simple problem to spot, especially if you are watching someone else make this mistake! Remember that the rod must come around on the D loop stroke in a flat, horizontal plane and then stay horizontal in the key position while the D loop forms. The forward cast then drives out on this horizontal, sideways plane. If you make the D-loop stroke and finish with your rod in the standard key position (at 1 o'clock and in a vertical plane) and then turn the rod 90 degrees during the forward stroke into a side plane, your front loop will nose-dive into the water in front.

Do not make the mistake of finishing the rod in the usual vertical key position and then rotate your rod 90 degrees during the forward stroke, as this will always drive your forward cast down into the water in front of you.

Make sure your rod finishes in the horizontal key position, having got there through a flat path on the D-loop stroke, and keep the rod tip path horizontal throughout the entire forward stroke.

CHAPTER 21

Sneaky Spey Casts

The spey casts are just as versatile and as capable of overcoming issues in front as the overhead cast is. In earlier chapters I talked about the use of the aerial mend, the shepherd's crook cast, the reach cast, and the slack line cast to overcome typical fly-fishing problems. In those chapters I described these movements as additions to the overhead cast, but many times you will not be able to make an overhead cast because of obstacles behind.

As in any other situation with obstacles behind, the easiest way out is to use a roll cast or spey cast to overcome this problem. As before, the spey cast you choose doesn't matter, be it single or double spey, snake roll or snap T. Use the right cast for the wind situation and your casting confidence and ability.

As you would expect from my earlier writings, I strongly encourage all fly casters to practice all casts and permutations, with both left and right hand, in anticipation of tricky situations that might be encountered.

I'm not going to describe each spey cast and each permutation of line management. If you took the four main spey casts and the four line management solutions (aerial mend, shepherd's crook, slack line cast, and reach cast) and combined them together, you would have at least sixteen casts. Then try them from the other side of the river and you would get thirty-two casts. That's a lot of paper—and a lot of reading time!

I will, however, demonstrate the four line management solutions with one spey cast—my favorite, the single spey. With a few photos and captions, you can see what needs to be done and then extrapolate these ideas into any of the spey casts you prefer.

Single Spey with Aerial Mend

Start the single spey as usual, but hold the fly line in your line hand with a loop of about three feet of slack hanging below it.

Make the D-loop stroke as usual, and ensure your line hand remains close to your rod hand and the slack loop is still hanging below your line hand.

Drive the forward cast out parallel to the rail track, and as soon as your rod tip has stopped but before any fly line has touched the water, let the slack line go from your line hand.

As soon as you have let the slack line go, move your rod tip in a horizontal plane in the direction you want the mend to land.

Before any fly line lands on the water, move the rod tip back in front of you. You want to ensure that the rod tip travels on a completely horizontal plane—not in a curve or a C shape—throughout the whole mending move.

The finished result is a nice curve in the line lying on the water and ensuring that your fly will fish for a short time without drag. Move your rod tip right to left to get a mend curved to the right.

Move your rod left to right to get a mend curved to the left.

Single Spey with Shepherd's Crook

Remember that the leader you use is as important as your technique in this cast. A long, fine leader will not work at all, so create a shorter leader with a steep taper to aid you as much as you can.

Start the cast as you would a single spey with side cut, making the D-loop stroke with the rod in a horizontal plane.

Start the forward stroke, again on a horizontal plane, keeping your hands close together.

Because you are going to bend the end of the line to the side, make sure you do not aim at where you want the fly to land, but where you want the majority of your fly line to land.

When the loop is at a point where you want it to kick and bend to the right, before it has unrolled and before any fly line has touched the water, give the line a short, sharp tug with your line hand.

The end result is that the fly line will land with the shepherd's crook shape. With a right-handed cast, it will bend to the left.

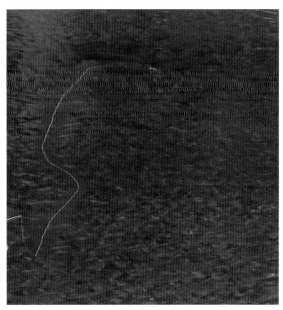

With a left-handed cast, it will bend to the right.

Single Spey with Reach Cast

Start the single spey as usual, forming a D loop behind you and opposite your target, ensuring there is a loop of slack in your line hand and that your two hands are close together.

Aim your forward cast where you want the fly to land, and make the forward cast with a front loop that unrolls in the air. As soon as the forward stroke is complete, let the slack line go.

Before the front loop lands (and while it is still unrolling), move your rod to the side.

Leave the rod on that side until the line has landed. The most effect will be achieved if your rod finishes 90 degrees to where your line lands.

The finished single spey with reach cast.

Single Spey with Slack-Line Cast

There are a number of ways to create slack in a cast, as I mentioned earlier. Again, I will not show every way. Just combine the relevant spey cast with the relevant slack-line cast to achieve the result you need. Below is the parachute cast version.

Make a single spey, complete with D loop and forward stroke, but again, ensure that there is a loop of slack (about three feet) held in your line hand. Aim the forward cast upstream of your intended target.

Before the forward cast has landed, let the slack line go.

Smoothly raise your rod to about 11 o'clock, still in line with your target, and before any fly line has landed.

Hold your rod high at the 11 o'clock position until the fly has landed.

Lower your rod tip at the same speed as the current to ensure a drag-free drift, but to retain enough tension for a fast, effective hook set.

I am going to come back to these Heineken casts again later, briefly, with what I think are the most satisfying of casts, the turbo casts. However, before I can talk about these (and before you can attempt them) an understanding and competence of the single and double haul are essential . . . and that is something I am going to cover in the next section.

ADDING DISTANCE

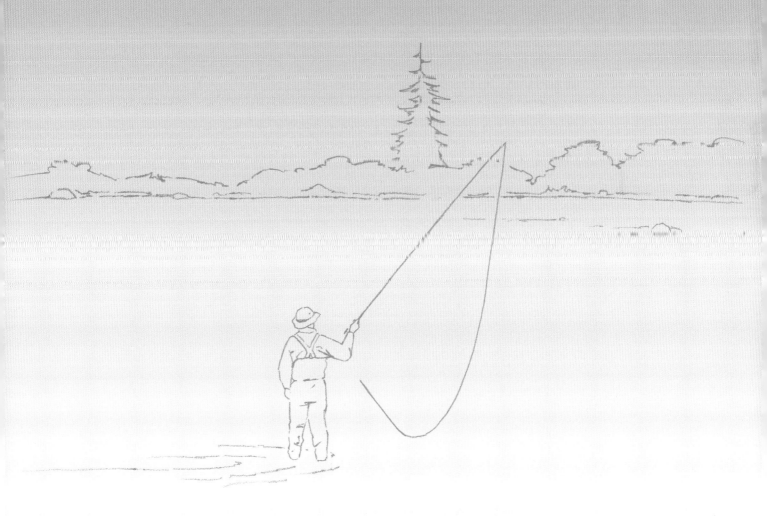

CHAPTER 22

Hauling

To-and-Fro Group

Most casters get to the stage where they need a little extra distance with their casts. Maybe it's because the fish are just out of range, maybe their fishing pal is casting farther, or maybe it is just time to improve their casting technique.

There are a number of subtle ways to increase distance: better timing, longer casting strokes, smoother acceleration, different rod or fly line, tighter loops, casting with a tail wind, and so on, but if you want to gain significant distance you need to learn how to haul.

A haul is a pull of the fly line, made with the line hand at a precise moment. The haul increases the flex in the rod, which in turns increases the speed the rod fires, which translates into more line speed. Though increased distance is the main reason most people haul, it isn't the only reason to haul. A higher line speed means you can cope with tricky winds, you can use less casting effort, and you can get a better presentation of the fly, as well as extra distance.

Of course, a haul isn't going to work if you do it at the wrong moment—timing is vital to the success of the haul. A haul increases the flex of the rod, so any haul must be timed to coincide with the rod's natural and maximum flex. This is during the power stroke of the cast.

If you look back at the chapter on the forward cast, you will see I talked about the ABC of the forward cast—how AB is the loading move and BC is the rotation and power application. The haul needs to happen during the BC. It is no good making a haul when your rod starts to move and finishing the haul before you get to the acceleration part—all this will do is apply two different power applications at different times (the haul and the BC). Instead, make sure that you apply a haul during the BC so that the two power applications work together and give you the line speed you crave.

Learning to double-haul is very easy. I would be surprised if it took a beginner more than thirty minutes to learn how to haul

(assuming they have an established cast) if taught the right way. If your regular cast is poor, with wide loops, poor timing, or no line control, don't attempt to haul. Master your basic technique first before taking this next step.

The easiest way to learn to haul is to set yourself up with a shooting head and attach it to a fine shooting line. I would recommend taking an old line, a little heavier than the rod you want to use. If you have a #5 rod, find an old #7 line (a #6 or even a #5 would do, but a #7 makes it very easy). Chop off the front 30 feet or so, needle-knot the back of this section to some 20- or 30-pound monofilament (a shooting line), and then tie a leader and some fluff onto the front end. Experience has shown me that this is a very simple and competent rig for learning to double-haul.

The best place to learn to haul is a park, field, or big lawn. Learning on grass is much easier than learning on water—you'll see why soon. So take your rod and new shooting head outfit down to the grass and get ready for all the comments you are likely to receive: "Caught any grass carp, mister?" or "You've got a long wait before the tide comes in here!"

Thread your rod up with the line, and make sure you have about three feet of the monofilament shooting line outside the rod. Cast the line out so it lands straight in front of you with your rod tip low, almost touching the grass, and pointing down the line. Now you are ready.

In preparation for the lesson, make sure you hold the line in your line hand with a good four to five feet of slack line pulled off the reel. Also ensure that your line hand is next to your rod hand, not apart.

My dad found the easiest way for a beginner to learn the double haul (for that is what we are going to look at here) was by numbers. No one can do four things at once, so do the four things in four separate steps.

To see how a haul benefits a cast, thread a line up your rod and step on the leader. Flex your rod against the line held tight by your foot.

With the rod held still, pull the fly line with your line hand and watch how much extra flex you put into the rod. This flex is what gives you greater line speed and why a haul is so useful.

Before you start to learn to haul, make sure you thread the line up through the rod rings and cast it out in front of you so that it is lying on the grass nice and straight. Your rod tip should be low, pointing at the fly line, and your line held tight in your line hand.

If there is any fly line inside the rod rings, or if the whole line is outside the rod but with no shooting line, you will have problems making the first few steps.

Conversely, do not have several feet of shooting line outside the rod before you start.

The perfect starting point is to have about three feet of shooting line outside the rod tip before you start.

The correct starting position leaves some slack line coming off the reel, and the line hand starts right next to the rod hand.

An incorrect starting position. Here there is no slack line between the reel and the line hand. The rod is also starting too high. Make sure the rod is low and close to the grass.

In this illustration showing the forward cast, I have finished the haul with my left hand, yet the rod is still bent and moving forward. This is a typical mistake with the beginner—the early haul nullifies the power applied by the rod.

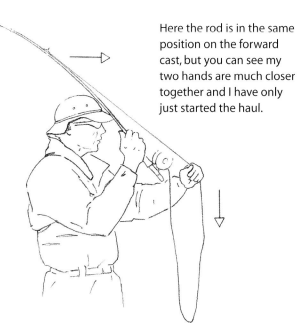

Here the rod is in the same position on the forward cast, but you can see my two hands are much closer together and I have only just started the haul.

Step 1

Make a normal backcast with the rod hand and at the same time pull the fly line through the rod rings with the line hand. Remember that there is a correct time to haul, which isn't at the start of the backcast. As I mentioned earlier, there is no point in adding the power of a haul during the loading move of the cast (the AB of the power stroke). The haul power should be applied with the power move of the rod—the rotation of the rod, the BC (see the forward stroke chapter).

Start the cast with a normal backcast, keeping the line held tight in the line hand and the line and rod hands close together as the rod lifts and starts to accelerate (the loading move). Keep your hands together until the rod has reached an angle of 11 o'clock or so. Now for the power move. The wrist and forearm of the rod hand kicks the rod back to 1 o'clock with a nice increase in acceleration to a positive and firm stop. It is during this power move that your line hand diverges from your rod hand with a smooth, but fast pull of the line. I'd say a pull of about three feet is a good start.

Once the rod has stopped at 1 o'clock and the two hands have separated on the haul, freeze. Do nothing. Just stay in that position and let the backcast fall onto the grass behind you. *Make sure your hands stay exactly where they finished.*

From the starting position, make a normal backcast but keep your two hands together through the initial acceleration and lift. When the rod is approximately at 11 o'clock, they should still be together.

Do not make the mistake of separating your hands at the start of the backcast. Here I have reached the 11 o'clock position, but my two hands have already started to diverge. This is wrong!

Without pausing at the 11 o'clock position, accelerate the rod back to 1 o'clock with a crisp wrist and forearm snap and stop the rod firmly. During this snap, quickly pull the line down with your line hand and stop that pull at the same moment the rod stops.

Freeze in this position, and let the line fall to the grass behind you.

Step 2

Keep your rod and rod hand dead still at the 1 o'clock position, and smoothly push your line hand back to meet your rod hand. The weight of the shooting head (and the lack of resistance of the thin shooting line) should pull out the slack line you are feeding when your two hands come together. For the benefit of the next step, it is vital that when your two hands meet, the line is still tight from your line hand to the butt ring.

Without moving your rod hand or the rod, smoothly push your line hand back to your rod hand until the two hands almost touch. By using a heavier shooting head and a thin shooting line, you will ensure that the line is pulled tight while the rod stays frozen.

Don't make the mistake of only half-sliding your line hand back to the rod hand. Compare the position of my left hand in this photo with the one above and you will see, here, that the left hand has not gone all the way back to meet the rod hand. This will give you a poor foundation to learn from.

Step 3

Step 3 is a mirror image of step 1. As before, start the casting stroke (the forward one here) by keeping the rod hand and line hand together throughout the loading move, and only start the haul when the rod accelerates through the wrist snap forward. Again, the haul must be fast and stop as the rod tip stops. Freeze in this position until the forward cast has landed.

Once your hands are together and the line is straight between line hand and butt ring, you can start the forward cast. As with the backcast, keep your two hands together during the loading move (the drive) forward.

Finish the forward cast with an acceleration of the rod to a 10 o'clock position, and at the same time, pull the line back down the rod with your line hand. Step 3 finishes with your two hands apart, your rod at about 10 o'clock, and your line hand down by your leg.

Again, do not start the haul as the forward cast starts. Here you can see I am still making the loading move of the forward cast, yet my hands are already starting to diverge.

Step 4

Once your fly line has landed on the grass in front of you and all momentum in the rod and line has ceased, push your line hand back next to your rod hand. You should now be back in the starting position and ready to practice the four steps again.

You might need to walk back a step or two or recast the line in front of you to get it straight again. Do not start step 1 again if the act of step 4 put some slack line on the grass underneath the rod tip. Straighten the slack in the line before starting again.

The final part of this cast is to push your line hand back to your rod hand and set yourself up to practice the four steps again.

The four steps are the four moves your line hand makes when double-hauling. The hard part is that while your line hand makes four moves, the rod hand only makes two. What is natural for most people is to move both hands together. Thus step 1 is not too tricky, but most people when they move their line hand back to the rod hand in step 2 also move the rod hand toward the line hand. This is a disaster for two reasons: 1) You are giving slack to the line when the rod is trying to flex. The rod cannot flex if you give it slack, so there is no load and the cast collapses. 2) If your rod hand moves toward your line hand in step 2, you have started a forward cast. Now how do you make a good forward cast when you find your rod is already halfway forward? The forward cast needs to start from the key position with the rod held back at 1 o'clock.

In step 2 you need to keep the rod hand in the key position through the entire push with the line hand.

All too common is to move the rod hand toward the line hand, giving a great wad of slack to the rod when it is trying to flex. This will give you nothing as a load on a forward cast, but this is very common in beginners.

I have taught hundreds of people to double-haul, and without a doubt, learning these four steps individually and with a shooting head like the one I described at the beginning is the fastest way to master it. Stop between each step so you can think through the next move. If you have never done this before, you will need to think about what to do next—believe me!

Once you have gone through these four steps a dozen times and are at the stage where you can do them easily, you are ready for the second level of learning, which is to put steps 1 and 2 together and 3 and 4 together. Instead of thinking about four things, you now only need to think of two.

Start the whole thing as before with line tight, rod low, and hands together. Make the backcast (step 1) as before, but before the line drops to the grass, push your two hands together (step 2). You need to do this while the line has momentum and the loop is traveling backwards. The momentum of the rearward traveling line easily pulls the slack line out that you are feeding as your two hands come together. Then freeze and allow your backcast to fall on the grass behind you.

The first few times you do this, I guarantee you will move your rod hand toward your line hand on step 2. Really concentrate on keeping that rod hand motionless and in the key position during the whole of step 2. Let your line hand do all the movement and stop with the line hand gently touching your rod hand, when the rod hand is in the key position.

The second level of learning the double haul consists of putting step 1 and step 2 together. There should be no pause of the line hand between the end of the pull of stage 1 and the push of stage 2. Make the backcast with stage 1 as before.

As soon as the rod has stopped in the key position, push the line hand back to the rod hand. You need to do this while the rear loop is traveling back and has sufficient momentum to pull out the slack. You also want to ensure that the two hands meet before the backcast starts to fall toward the ground.

Almost certainly, a beginner will make some movement with the rod hand toward the line hand and have the hands meeting in front of their head. Remember to make sure the rod hand stays motionless back in the key position (by your ear) until the line hand has reached it and the backcast has fully unrolled.

Your line hand really doesn't pause between the end of the pull (step 1) and the start of the push (step 2). I liken the line hand to a tennis ball bouncing: no sooner has the tennis ball hit the ground than it bounces back up. The same with the correct timing between the haul and the push; imagine your line hand is a tennis ball, and as soon as it has completed the pull, let your hand bounce up to meet the rod hand in the key position.

The second half of this level is adding steps 3 and 4 together, just as you did with steps 1 and 2. Again, your line hand does not pause between the pull and the final push—remember the tennis ball and you should be fine.

In this position I have completed steps 1 and 2 and let the line fall to the ground behind me. My rod is at 1 o'clock, my rod hand in the key position, and my two hands are close together. The forward cast and haul are about to start.

The haul and forward cast are finished and the front loop is unrolling in front of you in the air as you start the push with your line hand, pushing the line hand back to the rod hand. Again, this needs to happen while the front loop still has momentum and speed enough to take the slack line you are giving it before the front loop hits the ground.

Once the front cast has landed and your line hand has reached the rod hand, you are ready to start these two steps again. Practice, practice, practice . . . get the right timing dialed in at this simple level, and it will pay dividends in the near future!

The third level, and really the final one, is to put all four steps together. With the first level, you paused between each of the four steps—long enough to let everything stop and the mind think through the next stage before doing it. With the second level, you only paused long enough for the line to stop and turn and the brain to think ahead. With the third level, you don't pause. The thinking has been done before in levels one and two. Now the only thinking is before you start the cast.

The final level of learning the double haul is to put all four steps together. Make your backcast and pull and push your line hand before the back loop unrolls.

Just as the back loop has straightened (and before it has dropped to the ground), start the forward cast, pulling your line hand down to your knee.

Complete the forward cast with a long haul that finishes almost opposite the rod's finished position.

Once the front loop has unrolled and you have completed the forward cast, start another backcast (without stopping for the line to land or the cast to stop) with the correctly timed haul.

If you try and learn this technique with a regular weight-forward, you will find there is too much drag in the running line for the slack to be pulled out in this frozen position. The resulting loop of slack makes step 3 impossible to get right. Wait until your technique has evolved enough using the shooting head rig before you move on to the weight-forward and you won't have this loop of slack.

After this it is just practice. You have all the movements and timing needed to perfect the double haul.

I tend to let my students feel comfortable with this final stage using the shooting head and thin running line until they are able to make eight or ten false casts in a row, with correct haul timing and loop control. One thing I should mention is that your loop control will go to pieces when you first start learning to double-haul. Don't worry; it is easy enough to get the loops back, but let them be all out of shape while you focus on the importance of establishing some muscle memory in your line hand. When you can keep a series of false casts with the double haul going, you can then let your mind drift back to loop formation and tighten up those loops as you watch.

At this stage, it is worth moving to your regular fly-fishing outfit (which for most people is a weight-forward line) and practicing with this. After all, you are going to fish with this, so you had better get used to double-hauling with it. The main difference you will notice is that the line does not slip through the rod rings as easily when you are converging your hands together between each haul. This is because the running line is thicker and has more friction than the thin monofilament shooting line you learned with.

You'll get used to it. One trick here is to hold the line with only the tip of your index finger and thumb of your line hand. Feel the line tension in these fingertips when you are casting. Close your eyes if it helps (it does for many), and when you

have completed the haul at the end of the back- or forward cast, let the line speed pull your line hand back to the rod hand. This is very different (and much more effective) than just shoving the slack line back up the rod rings with your line hand and hoping there is enough speed in your loops to pull it out.

The hardest of all lines to double-haul with is a double taper, because there is no thin, running line, and the thicker diameter has more friction and weight. I'm a great advocate of improvement through taking more and more difficult steps, so if you want to really get good at double-hauling, move on to a double taper—after you are comfortable with a weight-forward.

If you do take this step, you will need to adjust a few things. Whereas a shooting head and a weight-forward have enough weight in the head of the line (and little enough resistance in the running line) to make three-foot-long hauls possible and practical, with a double taper this is not so, and usually the best effect will come from slower, smoother, and shorter hauls—maybe only a foot or two at most.

As you get better at hauling, I would recommend moving to a lighter double taper. A DT3 is much lighter than a DT6 and so has less mass to pull out the slack between each haul during the push. With the really light double taper lines your haul might only be six inches long—more a double tweak than a double haul, but it is still very effective at improving line control. Once you can double-haul with a double taper 1, I'll take my hat off to you and tell you that you have finally mastered the double haul.

Chinese Style

One additional tidbit of information I would like to share with you is casting Chinese style. My dad (again!) came up with the phrase and the idea, and I have used it ever since. Chinese style is no more than holding the rod at 90 degrees to the norm. Instead of having the reel hanging down, turn the rod so that the reel points out to the side and then cast. The reason you do this is that when a rod is flexed backwards (particularly with a rod lined with snake rings) there is nothing to hold the fly line away from the rod, so the line touches the rod any time the rod is bent backwards. This adds friction and drag to the line's progress, which matters little with a shooting head or a weight-forward, but with a double taper, and one as light as a DT4 or lighter, this friction makes the line stick to the back of the rod, and you cannot make a full feed with your line hand at the end of the backstroke. By turning the rod to the side, you actually ensure that the fly line does not touch the back of the rod and there is no added friction.

Admittedly there is a small problem with Chinese style, and that is the weight of the reel wants to drop to the vertical plane. One way around this was shown to me by Eddie Robinson, a great caster out of Utah. Eddie is one smart guy and has thought out more tips and tricks in fishing and casting than almost any caster I know. Eddie found the same problem when double-hauling and gets around this issue by twisting the top three joints of his four-piece rods 90 degrees to the side. With this method, you still have the friction drag reduced because the ring position keeps the line from rubbing against the back of the rod, but you also have the reel hanging normally and no off-balanced reel weight trying to drop to the normal position.

However, an added advantage of Chinese style (the original version) is that you can really lean against the reel face when you make a backcast, which helps gain a lot of extra leverage for picking up long lengths of fly line or adding power to a casting stroke. It takes a little bit of getting used to—holding the rod at this angle when it is trying to twist around—but it really, really works.

One problem with light lines is the drag against the back of the rod when the rod is flexed. See how much line is touching the blank here when the rod is flexed? With a light, double-taper line, this will prove to be too much resistance to overcome.

You will be able to haul fine, but when you push your line hand back to your rod hand, the fly line will stick to the rod and you will be left with a loop of slack between your line hand and your butt ring.

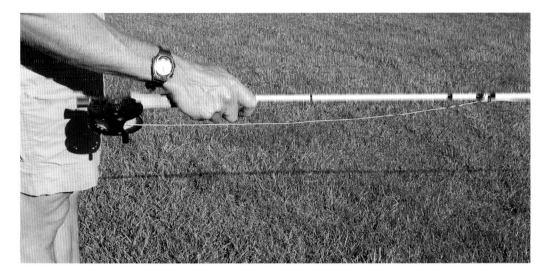

My dad taught me a technique that I have used for years and that served me very well in my tournament casting days. He called it Chinese style, though why I just don't know! If you hold your rod at 90 degrees to the norm, with your rod rings sticking out sideways, rather than pointing to the ground, you can overcome this.

With the 90-degree grip, the rod is taken to the side of the line so that when the rod is flexed as before, it is not in the way of the line; thus, there is no increased drag.

An alternative to Chinese style (if using a four-piece rod) is to make the top three sections of the rod 90 degrees and keep the bottom section, with the reel hanging normally, held normally.

So that's the double haul—a lot of words and photos and, I am sure, a lot of confusion. I don't know a better way of learning such a technique than having a physical lesson with a qualified and competent instructor. However, time, opportunity, and money sometimes rule the roost and a physical lesson is not practical. The next best thing is a lesson like this.

The double haul is a very useful and vital part of understanding casting techniques and, of course, improving distance and efficiency. As hard as it might be, I would recommend that everyone learn to double-haul and practice it until it is second nature and muscle memory has been developed—especially if you are going to read the next couple of chapters, which are all based on the double haul.

CHAPTER 23

Advanced D Loops

Continuous Motion Group

To be honest, I wasn't sure whether to put this chapter in the earlier section on problems behind or not. The information in this chapter is all relevant to the continuous motion casts, and it could have gone there. However, because of the advanced nature of the topic and because better control of your D loop will certainly give you more distance, I think that this is the right place for it.

This particular chapter was inspired after I watched an extraordinarily good demonstration of understanding D loops by two of the Northwest's most eloquent and gifted casters: Mike McCune and Scott O'Donnell. Indeed, I wrote this chapter while on the plane home from a Kaufmann Spey Days event that was held on the Skykomish River, with Mike and Scott's demo clearly reverberating through my mind.

Remember that the D loop is your load. It is what makes the cast efficient or not. Something that is worth knowing is what I call the power ratio (similar to, but not exactly the same, as the

Warning: This chapter is pretty intense and, I am sure, will be pretty confusing to a novice continuous motion caster. It is intended for casters who have reached a level of understanding and competence that would be worthy of a college degree!

energy ratio)—where the relationship between the D-loop load and the necessary forward stroke power equals 100. The essence of the power ratio is that you need 100 units of power to make a successful cast—call it percentage if you like, as that is probably more accurate. If your D loop gives you 80 percent of the load, your forward cast only needs 20 percent to succeed. If your D loop only gives you 20 percent of the load, then your forward stroke has to give 80 percent. That is the basis of this theory, and it works pretty well.

D-loop load comes from many factors: size, shape, speed, and line type in particular. I've already delved into D-loop size, so there is little need to go there. As to D-loop speed with regard to the line used, I'll cover that in the relevant chapter later on in this book. This part of the book is dedicated to D-loop timing and shape.

Timing

A perfect D loop needs to be directly opposite your targeted forward stroke.

There are three stages of the D loop itself: the travel, the stop, and the drop. When you stop your rod at the end of the D-loop stroke, the D loop continues traveling back (this is the travel), then stops moving as it runs out of momentum (the stop), and finally, with no momentum to keep it moving, will drop onto the water and stick in the surface film (the drop). A perfectly timed forward stroke should start just as the D loop reaches the stop. If you go forward while the D loop is traveling, you will rip the anchor out of the water and either hook the bush behind you or just have a bad hair day and a cast that frustratingly flops ten feet in front of you. If you start the forward stroke after the drop, you'll have too much line in the water and lose the energy you put into the cast as the line tries to rip out of the sticky meniscus—another bad hair day!

The perfectly timed forward stroke starts as the D loop reaches its stop.

If you don't start the forward stroke when the D loop has come to the stop, it will lose its momentum and drop onto the water, resulting in too much line stick, lots of spray, and a loss of energy on the forward cast (not to mention a dirty ripping noise as the line tries to break the surface tension).

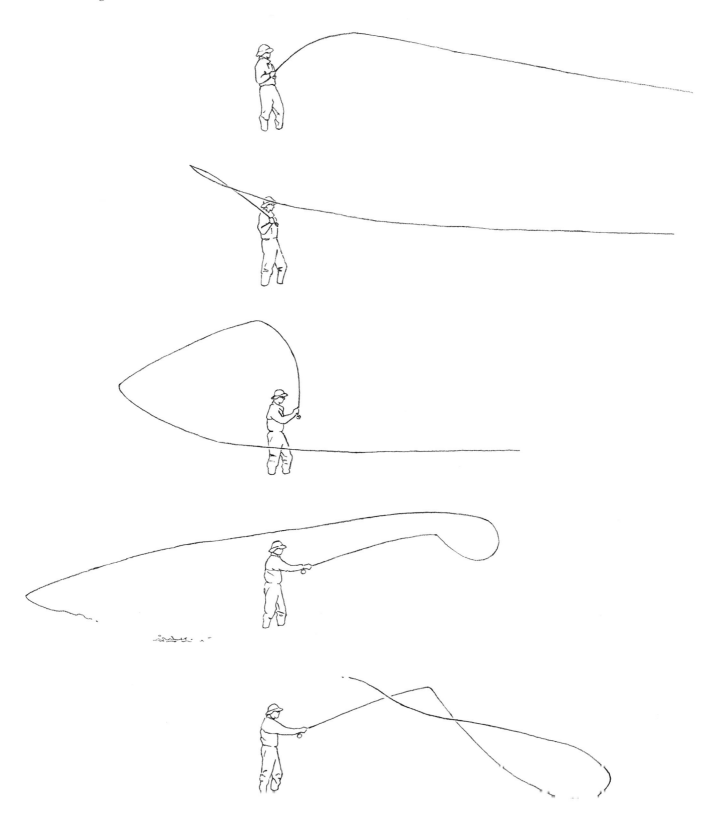

If you start the forward cast while the D loop is traveling back, the momentum between the two opposing forces will certainly make the D loop kick out of the water and crumple in front of you.

Shape

The best of all D loops is not a D at all, but a V or wedge shape, turned on its side. The narrow point of the wedge cuts through the air and has speed and load. The rounded D-shaped loop has great air resistance and little speed. Just like a forward loop, a good caster can tighten up this D loop and make it more efficient as a wedge shape.

A D loop is rounded and wide and has a lot of air resistance, creating a slower-traveling D loop and only a minor amount of load.

With a wedge shape, or a V loop, the thin nose is so efficient it cuts through the air with great speed, adding extra energy into the V loop and resulting in more efficient and longer casts.

A V loop is the gold at the end of the rainbow of the continuous motion casts, the icing on top of the cake, the dog's bollocks, the bee's knees . . . get it? The V loop is the best thing you could do to get the best casts. Period!

Alas, it isn't easy. There are a number of factors that control the shape of this rear loop and, while some of them are easy to control, one or two of them require a touch that is beyond that of a novice.

First of all you need a fast-action rod—something that flexes in the tip and not much farther down. Don't attempt to master V-loop control if you have a soft, deep-flexing noodle of a rod. The rod stop required to form these wedge-shaped loops has to be fast and instantaneous—not something a noodle can do too well.

Once you have the rod, you are on the right road. A V loop is formed using a flat rod path, a fast stroke, and a positive and definitive rod stop.

The flat rod path is probably the hardest nuance to master. Most of the time when making continuous motion casts, the rod makes a D-loop stroke and then finishes the D-loop stroke by rising to about 1 o'clock and the key position. The very act of raising the rod to 1 o'clock will pull open the nicest of V loops. Before we look at an illustration of this, think about what causes a tight loop on a normal overhead cast. It is a straight line path of the rod tip (along with smooth acceleration to a positive stop).

A V loop is formed with speed. If your rearward-traveling line is moving slowly, the bottom of the V loop can drop, and this will open up the V loop of its own right. This is the main reason that you have to have a fast stroke when trying to form a V loop (and also why you need a fast rod). The stop of the rod tip also has to be fast and positive. All a slow, soft stop will do is let the line speed bleed out and again allow the bottom of the loop to collapse toward the water.

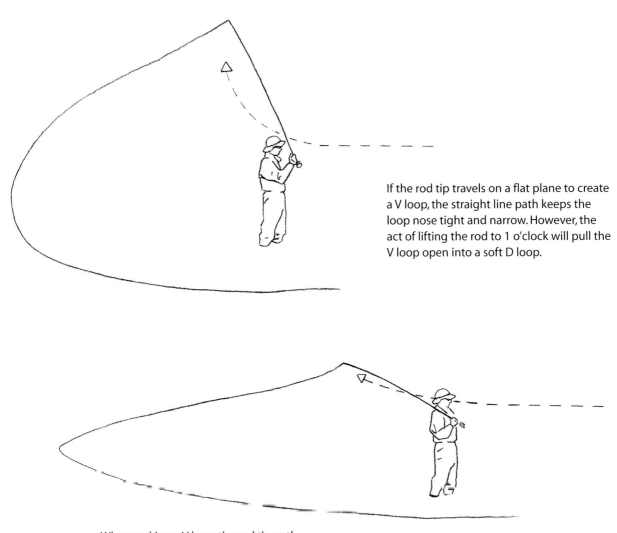

If the rod tip travels on a flat plane to create a V loop, the straight line path keeps the loop nose tight and narrow. However, the act of lifting the rod to 1 o'clock will pull the V loop open into a soft D loop.

When making a V loop, the rod tip path must be in a straight line with a lift of just a few degrees at the end. This will ensure that the V loop you have formed stays a V loop.

If the V loop has plenty of speed, the inertia in the line will result in the bottom of the loop staying above the water with a nice, straight bottom leg until the V loop is formed to its maximum.

When trying to make a V loop, I never start the tip of my rod higher than my chest—usually it starts about level with my belly button. The backstroke is fast, and the rod tip stays on that level, sweeping to the side until it is opposite my target, when it finishes with the slightest of rises. I rarely finish with more than an inch or two of rod tip lift, as more would open the V loop more than I would want. The rod tip reaches the stopping point and immediately and positively stops.

A perfect rear loop—the V loop—is a combination of a low, flat, and horizontal rod tip path; high rod tip speed; and a positive stop. A V loop like this has tremendous load and potential for the most efficient and longest of casts.

Regardless of whether it is a D loop or a V loop, the top leg and the bottom leg of the loop should be perfectly symmetrical when looking from the nose, or apex, of the loop back to the rod tip and down to where the loop is anchored on the water.

This shape is controlled by the rod tip path, and the best rod tip path is close to horizontal. At the end of every D- or V-loop stroke, the rod tip should lift some. This keeps the bottom leg of the loop out of the water and gives you time to make a good cast. D loops are formed by smoother, softer, and more rounded lifts, while V loops are formed by flat, horizontal rod paths with only the slightest lift at the end.

However, when forming a D loop, too steep an incline with the rod tip will give the loop an unnatural shape, with the top leg being more horizontal and the bottom leg having a steep incline. Scott and Mike call this shape the 7 loop because it looks like a number 7. The path the rod took created the diagonal slant of the 7, which has too steep an incline. It's a perfect description of this erroneous D-loop shape.

One shape of D loop that is wrong is the 7, which has a high and fairly flat top leg with a sharp, slanting lower leg to the anchor. The rod follows too steep an incline as the D-loop stroke comes to the key position. Usually this results in a lost anchor and no tension to load the rod.

The opposite of the 7 loop is the nose or schnoz loop (Mike and Scott again!). This D-loop shape has too much flat at the bottom. Again, the rod path creates the D-loop shape, and the nose is usually caused by the rod tip traveling too high on the D-loop stroke and then dropping down toward the water as the rod comes into the key position. The downward-traveling rod tip throws the D loop toward the water, resulting in this shape (as well as too much line drag).

If the rod travels too high during the D-loop stroke and then drops as it reaches the key position, you will get a D-loop shape that looks like a Roman nose. With a low, flat base, the D loop is likely to catch the water and drag. As you can see here, the apex of the loop is closer to the water surface and not in the center of the D loop as a good one should be.

If you are not too sure about the shape of your D loop behind (most people do not look behind them to check), have a friend watch and ask them if it is more of a D, V, 7, or a nose shape and adjust from there.

As with all fly casting, there are subtleties within casts and rod movements and, as I mentioned at the beginning of this chapter, the subtleties of the D-loop/V-loop formation are beyond most casters who do not have a clear understanding of line and rod mechanics. Not only this, but to fully embrace these subtleties and take advantage of what I have written in this chapter, you must have complete control of your rod tip during the entire casting stroke—and that is something that few casters truly have!

CHAPTER 24

The Joy of Slack (or Poking It)

Continuous Motion Group
Waterborne Anchor Subgroup

One undeniable fact in casting is that you need a relatively straight, tight line on the water in front of you before you make the backcast of any cast. Indeed, if there is slack in the line, the recommended solution is to roll cast the line straight before attempting to make a normal cast, as the roll cast is the only cast you can perform with slack in the line.

In some cases, slack is a bonus that can really improve the distance and direction of a continuous motion cast and particularly a waterborne anchor cast. You can certainly apply the following techniques to all the airborne anchor casts, but you will have to turn them into waterborne anchor casts first. More on that shortly!

The reason slack is a bonus is that when you make a D-loop stroke (with a waterborne anchor cast), the D loop is formed from the slack line in front of you. Take the double spey—when you have completed the setup stroke, you have laid the line on the water. The D-loop stroke brings the rod back over that piece of line, creating slack, from which the D loop is formed. That probably doesn't make sense, but here are a couple of diagrams that might help.

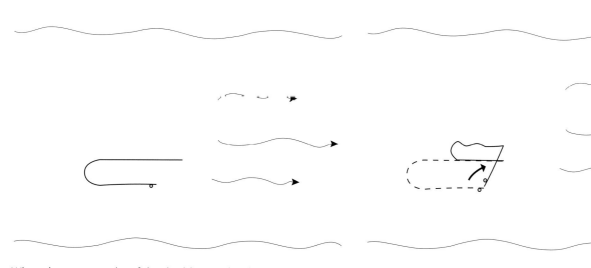

When the setup stroke of the double spey has been completed, the line lies on the water across your body and the rod tip remains pointing upstream.

As you sweep the rod around and downstream on the D-loop stroke, it sweeps back over the fly line lying on the water, creating slack. The D loop comes from this slack.

The same theory applies to the other waterborne anchor cast I discussed earlier, the snap T.

A good caster can enhance this principle to get more distance on a cast. Quite simply, the more slack in front of the caster at the start of the D-loop stroke, the bigger the D loop will be. You see, when you make a D loop, the D loop has to move backwards, behind you. If the line is lying tight on the water, there is a lot of resistance for the D loop to counteract. It is much easier for the D loop to travel backwards with the reduced resistance of slack line. The following illustrations point this out.

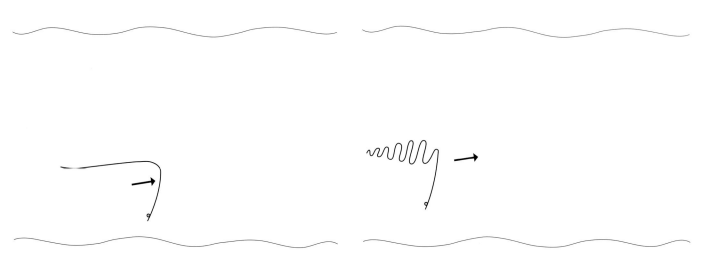

If a fly line is lying straight on the water, any movement of the rod tip away from the fly will have to overcome the drag and resistance of the line tension lying on the water. It takes more effort to move the rod against this tension. It also means that if you are trying to create a D loop against this tension, a lot of resistance holds back the D loop.

If the fly line lies on the water in a pile of slack wiggles, it is very easy to move the rod against this slack. The line doesn't have the same drag against the water surface—not until the slack is pulled straight. If, for example, in this diagram, the total length of slack that these wiggles created was ten feet, it would be very easy to move the rod tip back ten feet. Once it had gone back ten feet and pulled the slack wiggles straight, then it would encounter the same resistance and tension as in the diagram above. Creating a D loop against this slack is so much easier. The slack allows the D loop to travel back effortlessly behind you, until it is all pulled out.

Once you understand this principle, it is jolly useful to apply it in a cast. The best way to create the right slack is to dump a bunch of it in front of you before you make a D loop stroke. In Spey casting circles, this dump is called a poke. Once you have poked some slack on the water in front of you, you can throw back an effortless D loop. If you poke five feet of slack, your D loop will be small; if you poke twenty-five feet of slack, you will have a much larger D loop. So the key is to poke enough slack to create the biggest D loop the room behind you will allow.

The poke is a smooth, easy movement of the rod. In most circumstances, the poke will start with a high rod and drop toward your toes. You want the slack to be close to you. If you poke the slack too far out, it will land with tension—negating the advantage of slack.

Once the line has been poked into a pile of slack, you just need to kick around a D loop against the slack.

You can create a poke from either side of your body. If you are a right-handed caster, you can poke from your off (left) shoulder, and then whip the D-loop stroke to your right-hand side to complete the cast. Or you can poke from your right-hand side, and then stay on that side to create the D-loop stroke. It doesn't matter in terms of the effect of the cast, and I would recommend playing around with both for any cast you perform to see what is natural and comfortable.

A poke starts with a high rod.

The rod tip then drops toward the water close to your feet, dumping coils of slack in front of you.

A poor poke pushes the line out too far from the caster, resulting in tension, not slack coils. This would be good for creating a smaller D loop but not for maximum efficiency and distance.

A really good poke gives a lot of slack line in front of you. With this amount of slack, the D loop can be huge.

All that remains to complete the cast, once a pile of slack has been positioned in front of you, is to accelerate the rod around on the D-loop stroke and create an effortless, but energetic and powerful, D loop.

It doesn't really matter which side of the body the poke comes from. Here I am doing a double spey and have completed the first part of the cast, the setup stroke. Note that my rod is high and over my left shoulder. This is different from the standard double spey.

From the high rod position, I drop my rod down toward the water in front of me, creating a nice pile of slack to kick the D loop back against.

I can also make a poke from the right-hand side of the body. Here I am still making a double spey cast and have completed the setup stroke and D-loop stroke as normal.

However, instead of driving out my forward stroke against the D loop I have formed, I now poke the line back on to the water in front of me, creating slack to kick a bigger and more efficient D loop against.

As I mentioned earlier, you can also poke a cast with an airborne anchor—whether it is a switch cast, single spey, or snake roll. You would start the cast as normal and then, once in the key position with the rod at 1 o'clock and a D loop formed behind, simply dump slack in front of you and then finish with another D-loop stroke and the final forward stroke.

It may seem crazy to want to add an additional move or two into an already useful cast. For example, if you make a regular snake roll, you make two rod movements: the e-shaped D loop stroke and then the final forward stroke. If you add a poke to this cast (what I call the snake poke), you end up with four strokes: the initial D-loop stroke, a poke, a second D-loop stroke, and then a final forward stroke. So why would you do this?

Apart from the satisfaction of ripping out a long cast, or being a "castaholic" and just enjoying the pleasure of casting and adding components, there are a couple of justifiable reasons. First, all the airborne anchor casts are less effective with large flies, indicators, and heavy sink tips. Mass, on the front end of the fly line, tends to kick while traveling through the air. If you add a poke to any of these airborne anchor casts, you turn them into waterborne anchor casts and allow the water to grip the offending mass. Another reason for adding the poke to an established cast is that it really tightens up the D loop. By piling a bunch of slack in front of you prior to the D-loop stroke, you ensure that when you make the D-loop stroke the D loop will be directly behind you and lined up with the target. Without the poke, many casts will have a D loop that balloons to the side of your casting position, as well as behind—which is not nearly so efficient.

The most effective D loop is one that is tight to, and directly behind, you (as long as it is opposite the target). The poke helps to make this very effective D loop.

A less effective D loop tends to balloon out to the side of you, as well as behind. There isn't so much mass directly behind the rod from this D loop, so the rod will not load so well. This can happen on many casts, particularly ones that make a wide angle change.

Earlier I mentioned that the poke should come from a higher rod position, more of a vertical downward movement of the rod. This is certainly the easiest to learn and master, but it isn't compulsory. You can also create a great poke in front of you with a side movement of the rod, or a diagonal movement; it just depends on what you are comfortable with and where your rod happens to be when you decide to poke it. In New Zealand, some of the locals have developed a cast called the Tongariro roll. It is a continuous motion cast with a poke, albeit a sideways one. I have seen people demonstrating this cast off of a snake roll and a double spey—it doesn't matter what the start of the cast is, just that it finishes off with a sideways poke, then a ripping D loop and a powerful turbo forward stroke (more on that in the next chapter).

You can apply the same sideways poke to any of the spey casts, as you can with a more vertical poke. The end result is going to be similar; it is just a question of how much room is above you, what is smoother, requires less thought, and produces the best result for each individual.

I don't use the poke too often myself as I don't fish many heavy flies or indicators, nor do I need the ultimate in distance in my fishing situations. I prefer a cast with less moves and more efficiency. However, I have to say that when I feel the need for a rip-roaring cast, I will add a poke and a turbo (see the next chapter) and enjoy the easy distance those additions give me.

A cast that was developed in New Zealand for casting large nymphs and indicators is the Tongariro roll. It incorporates a sideways poke for maximum effect. The cast (here a double spey) starts normally, but as the rod comes around on the initial D-loop stroke it does not lift up to 1 o'clock but stays low and fairly flat.

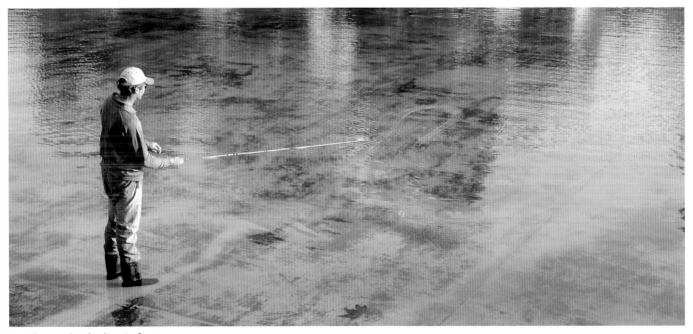

You then poke the line in front ...

…and a second D loop is kicked back against this slack.

Then you shoot out the final forward stroke.

CHAPTER 25

Turbo Casts

Continuous Motion Group

When to use this cast: changes of direction, obstructions behind, distance needed.

This is another part of the book that comes with a government health warning (as did the chapter on D-loop control!). To truly master the turbo casts, you need to have full control and ability of both the continuous motion cast you are going to add the turbo to as well as a perfect double (and single) haul. You can't expect to have the timing or touch needed for the turbo casts to work if you are still struggling to master a single spey. It would be like plucking a beginning skier still struggling with his basic snow plow stance off the beginner slopes and putting him on top of a double-black-diamond run in Val d'Isere.

So please, before you try these turbo casts, make sure you are comfortable with the continuous motion casts that you are going to add the turbo to. Ask yourself if you can do these casts with your eyes closed. Make sure you can cast ten in a row without poor timing; tailing, wide loops; or rushed casting strokes. If you can, then you are probably ready.

The turbo casts belong to the part of casting I talked about earlier—cast stringing. They are a mix of casts, combining one of the many continuous motion casts with a single, or a double, haul. I can't go over all the combinations of hauls and continuous motion casts or this book would never end. When my dad and I were teaching in Devon, England, we had a list of more than a hundred different Heineken casts, and we would teach a variety of students these casts as and when it was deemed nec-

essary. It was also important to teach these casts only to those casters interested in casting beyond the norm—casters who enjoyed the skill of casting as much (or more) than fishing.

One particular gentleman, Jack, was good with his skills and casting ability and a passionate learner. He would come down to Devon to be taught all sorts of casts. Jack sticks in my mind because one day we took him fishing on the River Torridge, and he used a turbo double spey with side cut and shepherd's crook (that's four different casts strung together) to land a fly under an overhanging tree and catch a cracking sea trout. To this day, that part of the pool is called Jack's bay.

I mention this in passing to illustrate the usefulness of these combined casts, but also to show you that there are too many permutations to list in one book.

So to get back to the turbo casts. They are continuous motion casts with an added haul either for extra distance, greater line speed, better line control, or to penetrate a wind. Some turbo casts have a double haul, some even a triple haul, but most of them have a single haul. These are the casts I have been waiting for! I don't ever make a spey cast these days without adding the turbo to it. The turbo speys are just too efficient and give the greatest, tightest, most desired, and drop-dead gorgeous loops of them all!

Single Haul

Cast your mind back to the basics chapter and the energy ratio. Remember, the less power you apply to a rod (and the straighter the path of the rod tip) the smaller the loop you will form. If you can use 10 percent caster power and get 90 percent load power, you will get the smallest loops. The fly line and larger D or V loops certainly contribute to increased load, but a haul gives you another 10 or 15 percent load, meaning you can really lay off the sauce and still zing out prodigious casts with seemingly nonchalant ease!

Most of the time you will probably use a single haul on any of the continuous motion casts. Remember, a haul increases line speed. You do not want this to happen on the D-loop stroke of a switch cast, for example, when you have trees behind you. Increasing the speed of the line in such a situation will only ping your D loop back with too much speed and ensure your fly lands in the bushes behind. Better to keep the power for when you need it—the forward stroke.

Because you are only making a haul on the forward cast, you want to hold the line in your free hand and make your D-loop stroke with your two hands side by side. Don't leave your line hand behind on this stroke. Apply a smooth single haul as you apply the power on the final forward stroke.

A good place to start to learn the turbo casts is with the roll cast. You don't have to have such precise timing as with the other continuous motion casts, and it is a good way of getting your timing right on the forward haul. As you get better and more masterful with the turbo roll, then move on to the turbo switch, turbo single spey, and whatever else tickles your fancy.

Most turbo continuous motion casts only have a haul on the forward stroke. Start the D-loop stroke with both your rod hand and your line hand together, and the line held lightly in your free hand.

Make your D-loop stroke as you would normally for whatever continuous motion cast you want to add the turbo to. In this case I am doing a switch cast to keep it simple.

At the end of the D-loop stroke, you should still have your rod hand and line hand close together.

Now make the forward stroke and add the haul at the moment of greatest acceleration with the rod hand.

Most casters I teach struggle with the timing of the forward haul and usually finish too early. Remember that the haul is only a power application and should coincide with the majority of the power application applied with the rod hand, which, if done correctly, is the final snap of the wrist.

Here you can see that I am halfway through my forward stroke and my haul hand has already started to move away from my rod hand. This is a sure sign of applying the haul too early and taking the power out of the rod, resulting in a slow and sloppy forward cast.

At the same stage of a correctly timed turbo switch cast, you can see my hands are still together—the haul has not started yet. The haul must wait until the rod hand accelerates through the power stroke. The extra line speed gained from this correctly timed haul will be very satisfying.

Some people find it easier to see the technique and the point of the lesson better with an illustration. This haul timing is one case where this can be a relevant point.

So the single haul is used on the forward cast of all continuous motion casts to get extra distance—all, that is, except those casts that start from a long way out and with a long haul.

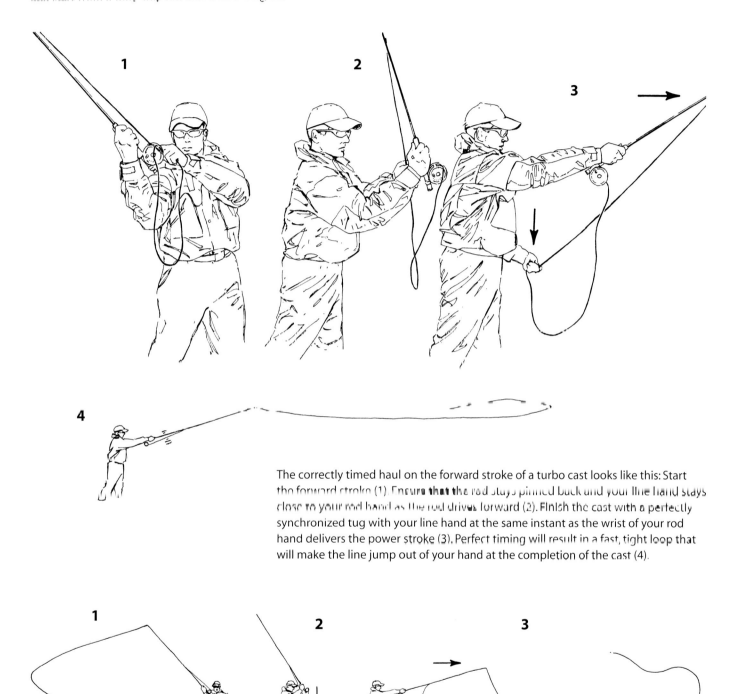

The correctly timed haul on the forward stroke of a turbo cast looks like this: Start the forward stroke (1). Ensure that the rod stays pinned back and your line hand stays close to your rod hand as the rod drives forward (2). Finish the cast with a perfectly synchronized tug with your line hand at the same instant as the wrist of your rod hand delivers the power stroke (3). Perfect timing will result in a fast, tight loop that will make the line jump out of your hand at the completion of the cast (4).

The most common mistake with the turbo casts is to finish the haul before your rod hand delivers the power. The forward cast may start normally, with your line hand and rod hand together (1), but the temptation to make the haul early and finish the haul before the power arc starts (2) will result in a slower, wider, and poorer forward loop (3).

Double Haul

If you are fishing with a long belly line, or better still a double taper, you may have to, or want to, make a turbo cast when you still have a lot of line in the water in front of you. This is where the double-haul turbo casts come in.

With a regular trout rod of 9 feet or so, the rod doesn't have the length to pick up long lengths of line on the water. Not only this, but if you have, say, seventy feet of line out in front of you and you try to make the D-loop stroke of a switch cast, you will find that you have too much line lying on the water to be able to break the surface tension. You just cannot get that much line out of the water with any degree of control.

However, by adding a haul to your D-loop stroke, you can use the extra load and power that the haul puts into your rod to break the surface tension. A smooth, long haul is more effective in getting a long line out of the water on the D-loop stroke than a short, stabbing haul is.

There is no doubt you have to be a better caster to be able to do this. First of all, you must handle much longer line lengths; second, you are casting double-taper lines (or at least long belly lines); but most of all, the D loop has to have tremendous speed. A haul is useless if it does not have enough speed in the rearward-traveling line to pull out the slack line you are going to feed between the hauls. It isn't too hard with an overhead cast, but with a D loop that is anchored to the water it is a different story. You must have enough speed in your D loop so that when you have completed your D-loop stroke haul, the D loop has plenty of momentum to draw out the slack as you bring your line hand back to your rod hand in preparation for the forward haul.

If you make a double haul for your turbo switch cast, you must have a long and smooth haul on the D-loop stroke.

To gain enough tension in the line for a good forward stroke, make sure you bring your line hand back to the rod and feed the slack line through the rod guides. To do this successfully, the D loop must have enough line speed to pull out this slack.

Take a look at how close my hands are in this photo as the forward cast starts. It is only from this position that a good forward haul can result. Also, look at the D-loop (or, more accurately, V-loop) shape. The wedge shape ensured I had high line speed and was able to complete the feed on the D-loop stroke, resulting in tension in the line at the start of the forward stroke.

The cast is completed with a long, smooth haul on the forward stroke and a release of the fly line. The wedge-shaped loop unrolling in the air is a good sign of a successful cast.

You can cheat by maintaining tension. Basically that means you need enough sensitivity in your finger tips to feel the tension in the line. As you make your D-loop stroke with a haul and then start to feed, you judge the tension of the line in your fingers and ensure you are never left with a slack D loop. If your line has enough speed to take the whole five feet of slack, you feed five feet. If the D loop is only going slow enough to take two of those five feet of slack, you only feed two feet, and if there is no speed in your D loop, you don't feed any line; you just keep your rod hand and line hand far apart and keep tension between the line hand and the rod butt guide. This is maintaining tension. Of course, if your line hand does not slide back to your rod hand at the end of the D-loop stroke, you'll have nothing left for the forward haul.

Once you can double-haul, or at least maintain tension with the continuous motion casts, you can really throw some very long lines indeed. It isn't easy—it's another step up the steep ladder of casting prowess—but it is worth it.

If your D loop is slow, you can cheat by maintaining tension. Here I have completed the D-loop stroke but only slid my line hand halfway back to my rod hand after my D-loop haul. The relatively slow-traveling D loop does not have enough speed to take all the slack line. Have enough sensitivity and awareness to feel the line tension and only feed what the D loop will take.

With a very slow D loop, or tight obstructions behind preventing a fast and large D loop, do not slide your line hand toward your rod hand after the haul. Maintain tension throughout the stroke. The D-loop stroke benefits from the haul, but without bringing your line hand back to the rod prior to the forward stroke, the forward haul is going to be quite short.

Triple Haul

In reality, you can put a haul into any casting stroke that creates enough line speed to enable you to feed the slack line generated by the haul. Why stop at a double haul? With a cast like a double spey, snap T, and even a snake roll, you have three movements of the rod, so put a haul in all three! I mostly triple-haul a double spey and a snake roll when using a double taper and when casting long line lengths. I use the first haul to get the line out of the water from a distance. The second haul creates a powerful D loop, and of course, the last haul sends the forward cast zinging out.

As with all hauling, you must have enough line speed for the feed in each step. I can't stress that enough. Failure in this department will lead to slack, and slack kills!

I use the single, double, or triple haul on all continuous motion casts, mostly because I rarely fish anything other than a double-taper line or a very long belly line, but also because there is something satisfying in casting long lines with limited backcasting space. A competent caster can pick up a rod loaded with a double-taper 5 and make a turbo continuous motion cast over ninety feet—with only twenty feet of room behind! I think that is something worth learning.

Only a few casts have enough rod strokes to make a triple haul. The double spey is one of them. Start the cast as you would a normal double spey with the line held in your line hand. As you make the first stroke (the setup stroke), make a haul with your left hand. This will help get a long line out of the water and make it easier to land the line tip in the correct position. The stroke must have enough line speed to take out the slack in preparation for the second haul.

If you have created a good setup stroke and have enough line speed to feed the slack before the D-loop stroke starts, you should have your two hands close together during most of the D-loop stroke. The rod (and hand) speed during the D-loop stroke will cause the excess fly line to flap behind the hands, but the line between the two hands must be taut.

Just as you start to accelerate the rod on the D-loop stroke, and before you raise it to the key position, make the second haul. Note that my rod is still fairly flat. You don't want to make this second haul with a steeply rising rod—all that will do is accelerate the fly into the bushes behind.

As with all the other turbo spey casts, use the speed of the D-loop to take out the slack as you push your line hand back to the rod in preparation for the third haul.

Finish off the triple haul double spey with a final haul.

TACKLE

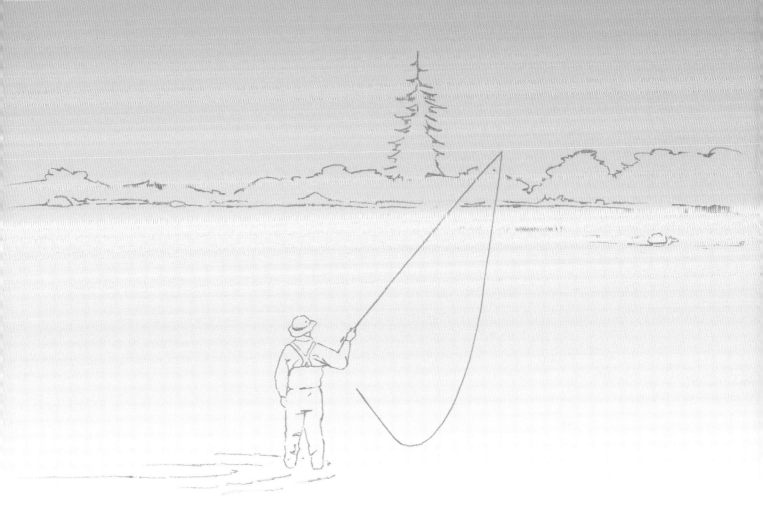

CHAPTER 26

Rods

This isn't a book on tackle, so I don't want to write a long piece on the finer points of the gear to use. But some critical things I think need to be mentioned here that will make these casts easier to perform or help you increase distance and efficiency.

Let's take a look at rods first. First and foremost, let me remind you that I am a caster at heart. I love casting, I love sexy casting—tight loops, high line speed. I like rods that allow me to do what I want. They stop when I stop, they move when I move, and every single movement I make with my hand is mirrored by the rod tip. So I use fast rods, light and tippy with plenty of power and stiffness in the bottom two-thirds. This isn't for everyone. Many casters need a rod that flexes deeper down, that is slower, that doesn't require such precise hand movements, and that is a little more forgiving.

This is never truer than when casting short lines in small streams and creeks. Most fly rods are rated and designed to handle a certain weight (measured in grains), and this is usually based on thirty feet of fly line. When you fish a small stream and can cast only fifteen feet of fly line, fast rods tend to be underloaded and harder to cast, and something a tad more forgiving would be a sensible choice.

However, being the caster that I am, I like this underloading. In fact, way before modern rods got fast and tippy, I used to use a rod two line sizes heavier than the line I fished with. My usual outfit was a #7 rod with a #5 line. That way I could feel the rod's speed and response. Nowadays I don't need to do this because top rod designers and casters like Jerry Siem at Sage, Steve Rajeff at Loomis, and Tom Dorsey at Thomas and Thomas understand this and produce rods fast enough. They also produce rods slower and softer for the fishermen (rather than casters) out there.

If you have great hand coordination, natural athleticism, and a sensitive touch, you will undoubtedly cast smaller and tighter loops and generate a higher line speed with these faster action rods. If you don't, these fast rods will feel clubby and underloaded. Better to pick a rod that will suit your own casting style rather than mine.

Traditionally, softer rods are recommended for roll casts and spey casts, and faster action rods are considered better for overhead casting. This isn't a bad way to look at rods for fishing purposes, but for me and my casting passion, I'll stick to fast rods for both!

I used two rods for the casting sequences in this book, both fast action. For the shorter line lengths I used a Sage 9-foot, 5-weight, four-piece Z-axis rod. For all my turbo casts and for the long line and tightest loop casts, I used the TCX series, again in a 9-foot 5-weight, four-piece model. Jerry Siem, the rod designer extraordinaire at Sage, painted them white to make them more visible in the photos. He used black thread for the whippings to give contrast and make it easier to see the rod flex and load. I think it worked pretty well!

Switch rods

While I don't want to get into detail about rods, I think this is a very good time to introduce something a little different. One of the latest trends in the casting and fishing world is the switch rod. These rods are a sort of cross between a single-handed rod and the two-handed rod of traditional spey casting.

A switch rod is usually between 10 and 11 feet in length and has a short cork handle on either side of the reel seat. It is a two-handed rod, but it is light enough and short enough to cast single-handed with a normal overhead cast. Most of the ones I use and like are in the lighter line sizes, from a #4 to a #7, so they are great for trout, smaller summer-run salmon and steelhead, and a variety of saltwater species.

They are worth mentioning because they give an extra dimension to regular casting. A longer rod gives greater distance, throws mends better, offers greater control when fishing a fly (particularly when nymphing in awkward current seams), copes with tough winds, enables casters to boom out long casts against a surf, and makes roll and spey casting easier.

Many people are starting to realize that they need the advantage the extra length of two-handed rods gives, yet they are intimidated by the full length associated with the two-handed spey rod. These switch rods are a great first step for those interested in using two-handed rods in a future life.

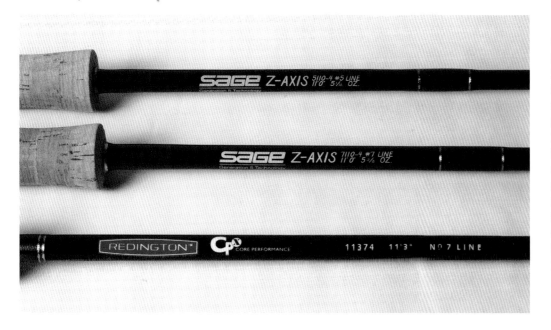

Currently my two favorite switch rods are Sage's Z-axis 5110, which I use for trout fishing in Idaho, swinging soft hackles and for streamers in the fall, and the 7110 in the same series. This is a fabulous rod for smaller river steelhead and summer salmon fishing, not to mention a great tool for fishing the surf for stripers and redfish. I also really like Redington's 11-foot, 3-inch, 7-weight, CPX switch rod.

CHAPTER 27

Fly Lines

If there is one thing I have learned in my time working at RIO it is that fly lines, more than anything, are one of the most important items of tackle when it comes to performance. Of course it helps to have a good rod or two; however, putting the right fly line on a broom stick can transform it and make it alive and very castable. The same can be said about a rod that is as bendy as a boiled noodle—just find the right line and that noodle becomes a nice fishing tool. Sometimes it is about the weight of the line and sometimes it is about the shape (the profile).

As I mentioned in the chapter on rods, I used to use a line two sizes lighter than the rod. This was because rods in those days (in England, anyway) were soft and slow and this was the best way to generate high rod tip speed. Many people overline a modern rod because they are so fast or because they fish them at short range. Line manufacturers take this into account and de-velop lines that are heavier than the official standard just to help the average caster load a modern rod that is too fast for them. Anglers alike are loath to break the rules. If a rod says it is for a #5 line, they must put on a #5 line. On some rods a #6 or even a #7 would be better, but they don't want to break the rules.

At RIO we take that into account with some of our fly line designs. We have lines that are in the upper end of the tolerances for the standard, lines that are slightly heavier than the standard, and lines that are quite a lot heavier than the standard. Of course, we also have lines that weigh what they should and con-form totally to the standard. However, it is interesting to note that (at the time of this writing) the most popular lines are all the ones that are slightly heavier than the standard. This is be-cause they load the faster modern rods deeper and feel nicer to most fly fishers.

Profile

The profile of the line is basically the shape of it—where it gets fat, where it gets thin, where and how long each taper is. As I said in the chapter on rods, this isn't a book about tackle, so I am not going to go into the advantages and disadvantages of each type of line taper or profile. All I'll say is that all my life I have fished and used double-taper lines, rather than weight-forwards. They are more stable at range, can be picked up at any length (whereas weight-forward lines have to be pulled back until the head is by the rod tip before they can be cast again), and if you are a good enough caster, they will give you all the distance you will ever need for fishing—even for a fly fisher ob-sessed with casting, like me!

There is no doubt that you cannot make an effective cast with running line outside the rod. If you have a weight-forward line that has 40 feet of head (fat line) and you make a cast that goes 60 feet, you will need to pull in 20 feet before you can make another cast. This is especially so with the continuous mo-tion casts. You can do this with either a double-taper line or a long belly line, and that is what I used for the casting sequences in this book. The majority of casts in this book were made with RIO's steelhead taper line—a weight-forward line that has a very long head and back taper, which is ideal for most people who want to make the spey casts, or continuous motion casts, with a single-handed rod. The really long distance casts were made with a Trout LT double-taper line—both lines were made especially for me in a bright orange color by Marlin Roush, the head of production at RIO, and his first class team.

In addition to castability and line stability, the profile affects how much line can be mended. Once the thin running line is outside the tip of the rod, you cannot throw an effective mend.

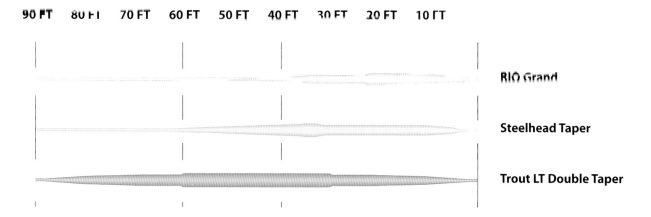

Fly line shapes are called profiles or tapers. Here are three standard RIO fly line tapers to get an idea of some of the basic differences that affect casting. The upper line is a regular weight-forward with a head length of 38 feet. This is a RIO Grand. The middle line is a Steelhead Taper from RIO with a head length of nearly 60 feet. The lower line is a Trout LT Double Taper. This line has no thin running line anywhere, which gives the caster a great range of line lengths that can be aerialized.

For smaller rivers and streams, this doesn't matter, but with long casts, controlling the fly and how it fishes in the water is integral to catching lots of fish. Again, this is where a double taper, or a long belly line, proves a wise fisher's choice.

As with my enthusiasm for fast-action rods, I must temper this advice with a word of caution. You do need to be a better caster to cast a double-taper line a long way. Most anglers—beginners in particular—will be served better with a regular weight-forward type line and the reality (and expectancy) of good fishing range casts, rather than tournament range casts.

Double-taper fly lines originated in the days of silk lines. In those days a line would only float when treated and dry. After fishing with a line for a while, the line would start to sink, so anglers would change the ends of the line round and fish with the other end. Modern fly lines float, so this is now not a requirement and the double taper is not seen as necessary.

Weight

There are so many things to say about the weight of the fly line that it would require an entire booklet to make sense of it. However, I like to make sure my students are aware of a couple of factors that can help or hinder their casting success.

The most important one is that you need to choose a line heavier for making a continuous motion cast than for making an overhead cast—that is if you want to keep a similar feel to the rod load. The reason for this is that when you make a backcast with an overhead cast, you have all the weight of the line that is outside the rod loading it. When you make a continuous motion cast, you have only the part of the line weight that is outside the rod loading it.

In truth, rod load does not need to be an exact amount, so you can still make a roll cast without using a heavier line; it would just feel nicer with more weight.

A fly rod is designed so that the flex increases as the line weight (load) increases. When casting with a short line, the rod will flex only at the tip and the casting stroke needs to be short. When lengthening the line length, the weight increases, the rod flexes farther down, and the casting stroke has to lengthen. When casting with really long lengths of line, the same rod will flex deeply down into the lower section and the casting stroke length needs to be extended even more.

This is easier explained with some numbers. If you take the AFTM standard for a #5 fly line, it should weigh 140 grains at 30 feet. If you cast a #5 line with only 15 feet of line outside the rod (because you are fishing a small stream), you will actually be using only about 65 grains (the front taper usually means that the first 15 feet of a fly line weighs less than the second 15 feet). It still casts on a rod labeled for a #5. When you go to the other end of the scale and use a long belly or a double taper #5 line and have, say, 60 feet outside the rod, you will be casting closer to 300 grains—on the same rod. Thus, the standard #5 you have can cast between 65 and 300 grains. It just loads deeper and you have to adjust your casting stroke.

There might be a sweet spot or weight with the rod. Let's say that you find your #5 rod feels really comfortable with 30 feet of line (140 grains). When fishing that rod on a small mountain stream and casting only 15 to 20 feet of line, it might be worth putting on a #6 or even a #7 line—just to try and keep your line weight closer to the 140 grains you are comfortable with. Alternatively, if you are casting a long belly line and like to carry big lengths, how about putting a #4 or a #3 line on the rod? (Again to keep the grain weight in the comfort zone—although this wouldn't be too good if you stripped your line in and had to start casting with 10 feet of a #3 line.) I'm just playing devil's advocate, but keep thinking about things and keep on your toes!

Finally, I want to mention something that is showing signs of crossing over from two-handed spey casting to the single-handed world, and that is a type of line called a skagit line (pronounced ska-jit). The skagit line was developed for casting very

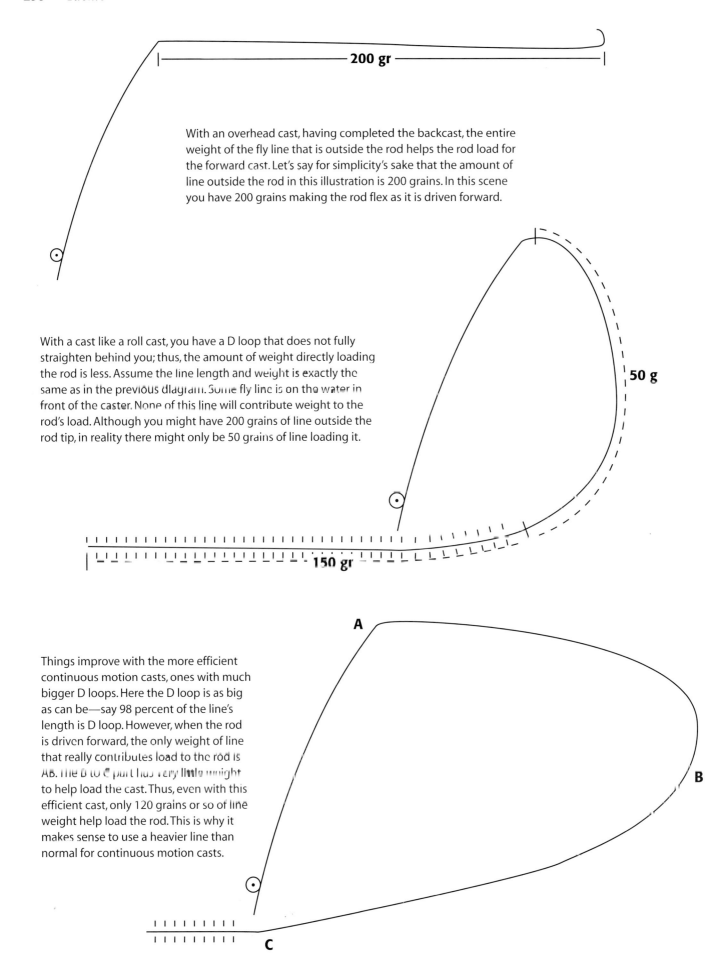

200 gr

With an overhead cast, having completed the backcast, the entire weight of the fly line that is outside the rod helps the rod load for the forward cast. Let's say for simplicity's sake that the amount of line outside the rod in this illustration is 200 grains. In this scene you have 200 grains making the rod flex as it is driven forward.

With a cast like a roll cast, you have a D loop that does not fully straighten behind you; thus, the amount of weight directly loading the rod is less. Assume the line length and weight is exactly the same as in the previous diagram. Some fly line is on the water in front of the caster. None of this line will contribute weight to the rod's load. Although you might have 200 grains of line outside the rod tip, in reality there might only be 50 grains of line loading it.

50 g

150 gr

Things improve with the more efficient continuous motion casts, ones with much bigger D loops. Here the D loop is as big as can be—say 98 percent of the line's length is D loop. However, when the rod is driven forward, the only weight of line that really contributes load to the rod is AB. The D to C part has very little weight to help load the cast. Thus, even with this efficient cast, only 120 grains or so of line weight help load the rod. This is why it makes sense to use a heavier line than normal for continuous motion casts.

A

B

C

Always put the line label onto your reel so you can easily recognize each line. All too few people do this.

This is a good choice of line for skagit-style casting with a big fly on a 6- or 7-weight rod.

SKAGIT SHORT LINE

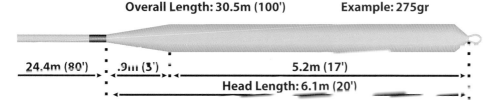

Overall Length: 30.5m (100')   **Example: 275gr**

24.4m (80') | .9m (3') | 5.2m (17')

Head Length: 6.1m (20')

A Skagit line really is simple in design—just a short heavy section integrated into a running line. The front of the heavy end has a loop for anglers to loop on the floating or sinking tip of choice.

Illustration used by kind permission of RIO Products Intl., Inc

large flies or heavy sink tips in Northwest steelhead rivers, such as the Skagit in the state of Washington. The line is simple in design, just a short, heavy section attached to a running line. No front taper, no finesse. It is not designed for finesse but for lifting weight and mass. In fly-line design terms the best way to make a fly line cast weight is to keep the weight (heavy fly) as close to the fattest part of the fly line. The skagit lines do this admirably by having no front taper.

There is so much mass in the front of a line like this that it will easily lift the biggest of flies and the fastest of sinking tips—things that are usually pretty tricky to cast.

As I said, this type of line is starting to appear in the trout and single-handed casting world. After all, it is not only the prerogative of the two-handed rod angler to use big flies. The right skagit line will make exceptionally light work of roll casting or spey casting the biggest conehead Muddler or heavily leaded stonefly nymph and the fastest of sinking tips—even on a rod as light as a 6 weight and as short as 9 feet.

As this is such a new topic in fly lines, here's a rough guideline of what weight skagit line will work on a single-handed rod.

#6 rod - 270 grains
#7 rod - 320 grains
#8 rod - 370 grains

Just be warned that with a standard trout/steelhead single-handed rod length of 9 feet or so you don't want too long a head on the skagit line. The longer the head is for a given weight, the lighter the weight of the line per inch. It is this weight per inch that is the critical factor. If a line weighed 300 grains over 30 feet, it would average 10 grains per foot. This is okay, but a line that had a weight of 15 grains per foot (a 20-foot head length) would have a much more useful lifting power.

Most single-handed skagit lines have a head length of around 20 feet, rather than the longer 27- to 30-foot head length that the longer two-handed skagit rods use. If you decide to try this, remember to add a tip to the front end of the skagit line. On its own, a skagit line will be too short to cast.

CHAPTER 28

Leaders

One of the most important parts of your tackle setup is your leader. Few anglers worry about this, particularly in the UK, where everyone I knew would fish a level leader of whatever breaking strain they needed.

What is the purpose of a leader? You'd be surprised, I'm sure. Many years ago my dad and I were commissioned to write an article on leader design for a fishing magazine in the UK. The editor of the magazine had been down on a course with us and was interested in some of the things we taught, especially some of the things we were saying about leaders. His brief was to see how short a leader could be, yet still catch fish.

We fished most of that season with leaders of varying lengths in an assortment of locations and for stocked trout, wild trout, Atlantic salmon, and saltwater species, such as bass (European Sea bass) and mackerel. To our surprise, we found that in terms of actually catching fish, leader length mattered very little. We used shorter and shorter leaders until we were using the very minimum length we could—one inch long with a small snap link so we could attach the fly. We still caught fish.

While such a short leader caught fish, it had a number of problems.

First, obviously, it was impossible to attach the fly. We had to use a snap link in order to do so. If you don't have snap links or other similar ways of attaching a fly, you need enough leader or tippet length to tie on your fly.

With such a short leader, it was impossible to get any depth with a fly fished on a floating line. We had to use sinking lines to get the depth we needed. This created problems when fishing nymphs and buzzers when a subtle line tip twitch was the only indication of a take. With a sinking line there was nothing to see.

The presentation was awful! With no leader it was impossible to get a soft presentation of the fly. The fly line would lash over and crash into the water—even with as light a line as a DT3. There was no way around this.

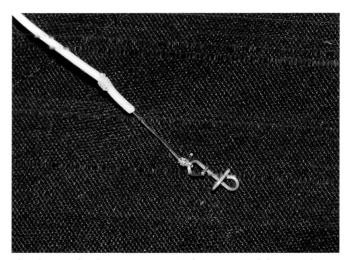

The shortest leader you can use is about one inch long, with a snap link on the end for attaching the fly.

The extreme speed of turnover of the line would snap off countless flies. A leader slows down the speed of the loop turnover. We got around this by using 15-pound tippet material for our one-inch leader, but this created a problem when trying to thread it through the eye of a small fly.

As I mentioned earlier, however, we still caught fish. Fish seemed to be oblivious to the fly line's presence. A lot of this was due to the fact that most of the time we used sinking lines, just to get the fly to a fishable depth. Anything that is within the fish's world is more readily accepted than things outside their world—think of divers swimming among fish. A floating line hovers on the edge of the world they know and their instincts treat this area with suspicion, thus with a floating line a leader makes perfect sense.

In addition, a leader's design is important, both for fishing reasons and casting reasons.

Casting

A leader should be designed to enhance the casting style and requirements of your day and should take into account three principle factors: the length, diameter, and taper.

There is no doubt that a big fly is harder to cast than a little fly. Big could be big, as in size, or heavy, or just large and air resistant. The easiest way to cast these big flies is to attach them to a thicker piece of monofilament. The thicker the monofilament is, the more rigidity it has to lift and turn over such flies.

I also use a much shorter leader for casting big flies. The main weight of a casting outfit is the fly line, and the closer to the fly line a heavy fly is, the easier it is to cast and the less kick there is.

Bearing both these points in mind, my standard leader for fishing unweighted streamers is a 7½-foot leader with a tippet of about 2X, or 10 pounds. When I change to a heavily weighted fly, like a conehead Muddler, I immediately change my leader, stepping up to a 0X (or even thicker) diameter and reducing it to 5 feet long.

In addition, I change my taper. The steeper the taper is in the leader, the faster it will turn over. A 5-foot leader tapering from 40 pounds to 15 pounds will turn over much faster than a level 5-foot leader of 15 pounds.

Another thought behind the taper design of a leader is what you are trying to accomplish with the cast. For featherweight presentation of a delicate fly, a long, very subtle taper is best. When you want your line to land with some slack, a very long, level leader is best. This could be for fishing a dry fly and avoiding drag, as mentioned in chapter 18 on slack line casts, or it could be to give slack to the fly to enable it to sink immediately—as Jerry Siem does with his unique side cast (chapter 14). To this extent a rule of thumb is worth bearing in mind: "The maximum length of level tippet material that will turn over

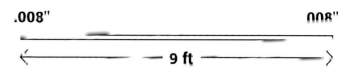

A level leader like this will turn over more slowly than a tapered leader of the equivalent length and tip diameter.

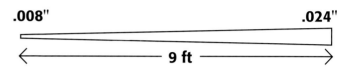

A tapered leader will funnel the energy towards the tip quickly, resulting in a faster turnover speed.

unaided and land straight equals one foot for each pound." For example, 4 feet of 4-pound material, 6 feet of 6-pound, and so on. If you want slack in your landing, exceed these lengths. If you want a straight presentation, stick with this rule of thumb.

A point to note: there are different stiffnesses and types of monofilament for which this rule of thumb doesn't apply, but it is a good guideline, anyway.

On the opposite end of the scale, a steeply tapered leader will turn over with speed. This is particularly useful when you are trying to get a cast to turn over very positively—if you are casting into a head wind, for example, or if you are employing a cast like the shepherd's crook cast (chapter 15) when you really need the kick and line speed to make the cast work.

Fishing

As well as casting needs, a leader's design should be carefully considered for certain fishing applications. Obviously you want a leader and tippet strong enough to land the fish you are after and the right size to perform the casting functions as described above. In addition, the taper plays a major role in how the fly fishes. When I was doing a lot of competition fishing, one reason for using a long, level leader was when fishing teams of nymphs and buzzers at depth. Weighted flies were not allowed and sinking lines just are not sensitive enough to detect subtle takes. The best way to get flies down deep and fast is to tie them on thick wire hooks, fish them off a floating line, and attach them to thin (4X, 6-pound) level leaders. A tapered leader has a thick butt section, which impedes the sink rate of the flies. A level leader has no such impedance and is far better at getting the flies down to the correct fishing depth.

This is also a consideration when fishing in a river with drag. The thicker butt section of a tapered leader has more surface area for the current to push against and affect the fly's drift. A thin, level leader will not have the same surface area or drag.

Although there are times when a level leader has an advantage, there is no doubt that in most casting and fishing situations a tapered leader will perform best.

Hopefully this chapter illustrates how important the design of the leader is. It is the least-thought-about item of tackle by the majority of anglers, but with the wrong leader design, even with the best rod, line, and casting technique, the cast can still fail.

There is more to making the perfect cast than being able to throw a tight loop, and there is, or should be, more than one perfect cast in every fly fisher's armory. As I said at the beginning, the object of this book is to open your eyes to the ways of casting a fly that can cope with obstructions behind you, in front of you, and all around you, and make it easier for you to fish the waters that other anglers frustratingly walk by.

aerial mend. A mend thrown into the forward stroke of a cast that ensures the fly line lands ready to fish. It is particularly useful with sinking lines and shooting heads.

AFTMA. Association of Fishing Tackle Manufacturers of America; the industry standard for line weights, measured at thirty feet.

aggressive D loop. A D loop that has its own weight and momentum to load the rod.

airborne anchor. A group of continuous motion casts in which the fly line travels back through the air while the D loop is formed.

anchor. The grip on the fly line caused by the water surface tension between the D loop and forward stroke of a continuous motion cast.

backhanded. Making a cast with the rod held in the left hand and angled on the right side of the body, or in the right hand angled on the left side.

bloody L. An anchor that lies on the water in a curved or L shape.

cast stringing. The act of putting together part (or parts) of one cast and adding it to part (or parts) of another cast to create a new one.

casting stroke. A deliberate stroke of the rod designed to maneuver the fly line during a cast.

catch cast. A cast that enables the angler to catch the leader or line tip in his hand.

collision loop. An incorrect loop formed on a forward stroke that collides with itself, caused by the backcast and forward cast not being opposite each other.

continuous motion. A group of casts that have a backcast that forms below the rod tip, which anchors on the water level, or in front of the caster.

creep. A casting error when the caster does not hold the rod tip motionless while the backcast finishes but edges forward while the backcast is moving.

crude spey. A basic and original form of the single spey with little efficiency.

crumpled anchor. An anchor that lies on the water in a crumpled pile of slack; also known as a piled anchor.

dangle. In a river, when the fly line has swung directly downstream of the angler and can swing neither left or right.

D loop. The back loop of a continuous motion cast that hangs below the rod tip and is anchored on the water in front of, or level with, the caster.

D-loop stroke. The casting stroke that forms the D loop.

double haul. A casting technique that has two hauls.

double roll. An advanced form of the roll cast.

double spey. A traditional continuous motion cast that uses two particular casting strokes prior to the forward stroke. Part of the waterborne anchor group of casts.

double taper. A fly line profile that consists of a level line with an equal taper at either end.

downstream wind. A wind that blows downstream with the current.

drag. The effect a current has on a fly line, leader, or fly that prevents it from drifting naturally at the same speed and in the same path as the current.

dry-fly spey. A type of continuous motion cast that is used when fishing a dry fly and with obstructions behind.

energy ratio. The ratio between the amount of load and flex in the fly rod derived from the weight and energy of the fly line against the amount of power required by the caster's effort to perform a cast.

feed. Part of the double haul referring to the act of pushing the slack line held in the line hand back to the rod hand between two hauls and while the cast is still in motion.

forward spey. Another term for the switch cast.

forward stroke. A casting stroke that delivers the line in front of the caster.

haul. A pull of the fly line during a casting stroke that increases the flex of the rod and the power of the cast.

head. A term for the fattest, and front, part of a fly line profile.

Heineken casts. A nickname for a group of casts formed by cast stringing.

key position. The correct position of the rod hand when it is motionless between a backstroke and a forward stroke.

left bank. The left side of the river when looking downstream.

loop. The shape the fly line takes when a casting stroke has been completed.

mend. A curve in the fly line that an angler deliberately puts in to counteract the ill effect of a current.

modern spey. A modern version of the single spey.

negative curve cast. A cast, usually made on a horizontal plane, that ensures the fly line lands on the water with a curve. Caused by decelerating the loop speed to make the line collapse into the curve shape.

overhead cast. A cast that has the rod on both the backstroke and the forward stroke in a vertical plane and where the line unrolls above the rod tip between each stroke.

parachute cast. A cast that delivers slack into the fly line and aids a drag-free drift of a fly, usually used when fishing a dry fly downstream.

passive D loop. A D loop that only has its own weight to load the rod.

pirouette. The term for the rotation of the fly or line tip between the D-loop stroke and the forward stroke of a waterborne anchor cast.

piled anchor. An anchor that lies on the water in a crumpled pile of slack; also known as a crumpled anchor.

point P. The exact spot where the D loop meets the water on a continuous motion cast.

poke. A movement of the rod, prior to the D-loop stroke, designed to create slack on the water and in front of the caster.

positive curve cast. A cast, usually made on a horizontal plane, that ensures the fly line lands on the water with a curve. Caused by accelerating the loop speed to make the line kick into the curve shape.

power ratio. A ratio of power that illustrates the effectiveness of each continuous motion cast. It assumes the total power required to make a good cast equals 100 and refers to the ratio between the load achieved by a D-loop power and the required power for a successful forward stoke.

profile. The shape of a fly line.

rail tracks. A term for two imaginary lines that are the essence of success in the continuous motion casts. One rail track is the anchor and the other is the direction in which the forward stroke should be aimed.

reach cast. A version of a cast that redirects the fly line, and not the fly, before the final cast lands on the water.

right bank. The right side of the river when looking downstream.

rod flex. The bend of a rod.

rod load. The mass that makes the rod bend.

roll cast. One of the continuous motion casts that does not change direction.

roll cast with side cut. A roll cast that delivers the forward cast on a horizontal plane instead of a vertical plane.

running line. The thin fly line behind the head on a weight-forward type fly line that aids this line in achieving distance.

setup stroke. A casting stroke that precedes a D-loop stroke on a continuous motion cast, usually on the double spey and snap T or snap C casts.

shepherd's crook. A cast, usually made on a horizontal plane, that ensures the fly line lands on the water with a curve; also known as a positive curve cast or negative curve cast.

shooting head. A fly line, usually short, that is independently connected to a shooting line.

shooting line. A thin line that has little drag or weight that attaches to a shooting head and allows for casts of great distance.

side cast. A to-and-fro cast made on a horizontal plane.

side cut. An act during a casting stroke (usually a forward stroke) that rotates the rod from a vertical plane to a horizontal plane.

side roll. Another term for the roll cast with side cut.

side spey. A continuous motion cast with a forward loop that unrolls on a horizontal plane.

single haul. A single pull of the fly line during a casting stroke, designed to increase the rod flex and load.

single spey. A traditional continuous motion cast that uses one particular casting stroke prior to the forward stroke and that has an airborne anchor.

skagit line. A type of fly line that is short and heavy and designed for casting heavy sink tips and flies with ease.

slack-line cast. A version of a cast that delivers slack into the fly line or leader and aids in a drag free drift of the fly.

snake roll. A modern continuous motion cast in the airborne anchor family.

snap C. A modern continuous motion cast in the waterborne anchor family.

snap T. A modern continuous motion cast in the waterborne anchor family.

spey cast. A style of continuous motion cast that changes direction.

splash and go. A term for the correct timing of an airborne anchor cast.

steeple cast. A type of to-and-fro cast that is supposed to send the backcast vertically in the air above the caster and the forward cast out in front.

stick. Another term for anchor.

switch cast. A traditional continuous motion cast in the airborne anchor family that does not change direction.

tailing loop. A loop that crosses and catches on itself during a casting stroke, usually resulting in a wind knot.

tempo. The speed and rhythm at which the rod travels throughout a casting stroke.

timing. The length of time between each casting stroke.

to and-fro casts. A group of casts that have a backcast that forms above the rod tip, which unrolls entirely in a straight line and never touches the water before the forward cast is made.

Tongariro roll. A type of continuous motion cast developed in New Zealand that incorporates a poke and a turbo to cast big flies and indicators easily.

traditional spey. An older and more traditional version of a single spey, which is less efficient than the modern spey.

turbo. Putting a haul into a continuous motion cast.

turbo spey. A type of continuous motion cast that has one haul or more.

turnover. The act of a loop that unrolls fully to a straight line before it lands on the water.

upstream wind. The term for a wind that blows upstream against the current.

V loop. A type of D loop that is not rounded but wedge shaped and highly efficient.

waterborne anchor. A group of continuous motion casts in which the fly line remains on the water while the D loop is formed.

weight-forward. A fly line profile that has a heavier and fatter head at one end that seamlessly integrates into a thin running line.

ACKNOWLEDGMENTS

It is impossible to list here all the people who have helped and influenced me—there are just too many. A big thanks goes to Chad and Lonnie Allen at Three Rivers Ranch in Idaho for allowing me access to their beautiful private section of Robinson Creek for some of the photos in this book. The rest of this book was shot on the Warm River outside Ashton and the Snake River near Idaho Falls. My great friend Kevin Bell, a professional photographer in California, shot the photos for the Joy of Slack chapter on the casting pond at the Long Beach Casting Club.

My dad, who was one of the finest fly-casting instructors in the world, had a great saying: "There is no such thing as a stupid student, just a stupid instructor." I love that phrase and try to live by it. As an instructor, it is my job to say the right words to my students to make them understand and to help them learn—there is always a way through, I just have to find it!

There are many people I have learned from, both casting techniques and teaching techniques (which are very different). My dad, obviously, was my early mentor and taught me the very best things in life. I was also lucky enough to be taken under the wing of Howard Tonkin, a lovely man from the West Country of England, who was the first person to get me (and my dad) interested in tournament casting. Guido Vink was a tournament caster from Belgium and a great one at that. He also spent a lot of time teaching a young Englishman some of the more advanced tournament casting techniques.

I grew up in England surrounded by other great casters, demonstrators, and instructors, and their abilities and influence are part of my life, techniques, and teachings. Charles Jardine has always been there for me; Nick Hart, Ian Gordon, Gary Coxon, Andy Murray, Eion Fairgrieves, Derek Brown, Hywel Morgan, Scott McKenzie, Gordon Armstrong, Paul Arden, Gary Scott, Robin Gow, and Robin Elwes are just a few who I respect and from whom I have learned. One name not in this list is the late Alex Henderson. Few people knew Alex, but I was lucky enough to work with him and have him work with and teach for me. He was a natural teacher and a wonderful caster—one of the best I have ever met, and his ability to put students at ease during his lessons was second to none. I shall always miss Alex, who passed away much too young.

In the rest of the world I have had many influences: Tim Rajeff is a person who fly casters would do well to emulate. He is an incredible caster, a gifted instructor, a truly great demonstrator, and an out-and-out nice person. His patience, analogies, and anecdotes—not to mention prodigious casting talent—are awe-inspiring. The late Mel Krieger showed incredible enthusiasm, passion, and entertainment in his teachings, writings, and demonstrations—an absolute giveaway of a great and successful instructor. Exactly the same can be said of Lefty Kreh—someone whose love of the sport shines through and another outstandingly good instructor, author, and demonstrator. I can't forget Ed Jaworowski, Mike and Denise Maxwell, Don Hogan, Ed Ward, Al Buhr, Scott O'Donnell, Joan Wulff, Way Yin, Mike McCune, Steve Choate, Nobuo Nodera, Steve Rajeff, Bruce Richards, Rick Hartman, Gary and Jason Borger, Mike Lawson, Cathy Beck, and Nick Curcione. These people are all (rightly) held as masters of their sport, and any aspiring teacher, demonstrator, or fly caster will do well to follow their paths through the professional fly-fishing life.

Jim Vincent and his wife Kitty, asked me to work for them at RIO back in the late 1990s. Without them, I would never have moved to the United States and would never have met some of the greatest fly fishers and casters in the world. I owe Jim a second thanks for his wonderful camera work with this book and for missing hours of hunting to patiently snap the images I believed were necessary! Greg Pearson, my spey amigo, who not only is the fabulous illustrator of this book, my first book, and countless others, but also is an incredibly likeable man, with great casting ability and unbelievable teaching skills. I am the fortunate one when he says, "Yes, I will teach that class with you."

At RIO I have to thank Marlin Roush and Jake Holm for pandering to my whims and building me some very special lines for this book, as well as John Harder and my great friend Zack Dalton—I owe them both more than I can ever say, in work, in advice, in friendship, and in fishing. I value these fine chaps and relish their company. At Sage, Marc Bale, Travis Campbell, and of course Jerry Siem—to these gentlemen I owe a tremendous debt of gratitude. Travis and Marc are among the industry's finest people and have taught me so much and freely given advice and time to me when needed—not to mention shown patience to an inept marketing man! Jerry is a whiz, and it is impossible to voice my thanks strong enough here—I just don't have the words. Jerry is one of the finest casters I have ever met, and I have gleaned tips and tricks from him at every opportunity possible. He has always been there for me and my strange requests, not least when I asked him to make me the two white rods for this book.

In my evolution as caster and instructor, student and fisherman, retailer and consultant, I have come across countless industry folk who helped me—for no gain or fame. At Daiwa I worked with Steve McCaveny, John Middleton, and Nobuo Nodera. At Thomas and Thomas with Tom Dorsey, Trevor Bross, and Lon Deckard, and at Frontiers with Tarquin Millington-Drake, Molly Fitzgerald, and Mike Fitzgerald. Thanks also go to Peter Crow at Action Optics; Shelley Thornton, first at Action Optics, then at Mountain Khakis; Yvon Chouinard and Bill Klyn at Patagonia; Shannon Robinson and Ryan Harrison at Waterworks. All these folks have helped me in my life, and it really does make me believe that the world isn't such a bad place after all.

No acknowledgement would be complete without thanking Judith Schnell at Stackpole Books for having faith in me and persuading me that I could write something that people would want to read. Thanks to Judith and her team, particularly Amy Lerner, for the hours of editing they must have spent translating my scratchings and scribblings into English.

I have been fortunate enough to fish in many, many places around the world and thanks for such opportunities must be shown to my great friend Hans Terje Anonsen and his wonderful family, to Bo Ivanovic, Alan Williams, Jan Sjaastad, Derek and Peter Kyte, Bill Greiner, Wes Webb, Federico Prato, Drew Montague, Vicky and Rick Nunn, and countless guides and gillies who have taken me fishing just for the hell of it!

I want to mention three very special friends, fly fishers that I hold in the very highest regards. The first is Rich Nickell, a great chum and collaborator, the best man at my wedding, and a very fine fly fisher. Rich runs Blakewell Fishery in Barnstaple in North Devon. Then there is John Horsey from Bristol—another great mate and exceptionally gifted fly fisher who has fished for England on several occasions. Finally there is Iain Barr—truly a soul spirit of mine and with whom I have shared so many laughs and good times. Now that I live in the United States, I miss these lads and their company tremendously.

Aside from casting and teaching techniques, there are plenty of reasons to be grateful to the many influences in my life. My wife, Susan, and children, Chloe and Tristan, are the best. They complete me and make my life the enjoyment it is. Much as I love my fly fishing (and fly casting), these pale in insignificance when compared to spending time with my family. For them I try to be a better man.

I know I have mentioned my dad already and his professional influence on my life, but without the influence, guidance, love, and support of both he and my stepmum, Smum, I would be a different person—probably an air force pilot in the RAF! My mum and stepdad, Arthur, I also love tremendously and admire their passion for life and the great outdoors. Their outlook, respect, and love for the natural world is a major influence in my life.

As always with these acknowledgments, I have probably rambled on too long. I have also, certainly, forgotten a number of people who have had a major impact on my fly-fishing life and who deserve to be mentioned here. This book is a result of what I have learned from other people, and if their names are not here it is not because I didn't value their help and guidance, it's because I write this late at night, with a glass of single malt nearly finished and a tired brain trying to blow the mists of time away.

acceleration, defined, 4–5
  See also under individual casts
aerial mend, 160, 180
  defined, 242
  fault finding, 154
  forward cast, 152, 153
  single spey with, 181–183
  technique, 149–154
  when to use, 149
AFTMA, 242, 237
airborne anchor casts, defined, 9, 242
anchor
  See also under individual casts
  airborne, defined, 9, 242
  bloody L, defined, 66, 242
  crumpled (piled), defined, 242
  defined, 9, 242

backhanded, defined, 242
backstroke. *See* D-loop stroke
bloody L, defined, 66, 242
  See also under individual casts
Bray, the River, 117
  Black Pool, 47

Cape Cod, 31
casting stroke, defined, 242
Casting with Lefty Kreh (Kreh), 162
cast stringing, defined, 171, 242
catch cast
  defined, 242
  technique, 13–16
  when to use, 13
circle C. *See* snap T
circle spey. *See* snap T
collision loop, defined, 67, 242
  See also under individual casts
continuous motion casts, defined, 9, 242
creep/creeping, defined, 45, 242
  See also under individual casts
crude spey. *See* single spey, crude
crumpled (piled) anchor, defined, 242
C spey. *See* Snap T

dangle, defined, 242
D loop
  See also under individual casts
  aggressive, defined, 242
  defined, 242
  passive, defined, 242
D loop, advanced
  overview of, 208–210
  shape, 211–214
  timing, 208

D-loop stroke (backstroke), defined, 9, 242
  See also under individual casts
Dorsey, Tom, 234
double haul
  defined, 242
  turbo cast, 228–230
double roll cast
  anchor, 32
  backstroke (D-loop stroke), 32, 33
  defined, 242
  D loop, 32–34
  forward stroke, 32–34
  key position, 33
  technique, 32–34
  when to use, 32
double spey, 88, 100, 171, 215, 219, 220,
      222, 231
  anchor, 75, 78, 84, 85, 114
  backstroke (D-loop stroke), 69, 73–80, 83,
      85, 86, 104, 106
  bloody L, 75, 78, 84, 85, 114
  collision loop, 87
  defined, 242
  D loop, 73–75, 81, 82, 87, 172
  fault finding, 84–87
  forward stroke, 69, 75–85, 87
  point P, 70, 71
  rail tracks, 75, 78, 84, 87
  setup stroke, 69–73, 76, 77, 81, 82, 84, 85
  technique, 68–87
  what hand to use, 68, 69
  when to use, 68
double taper, defined, 242
downstream wind, defined, 242
drag, defined, 242
dry-fly spey
  anchor, 121–123
  backstroke (D-loop stroke), 117, 118, 120,
      123
  defined, 242
  D loop, 122, 124
  false casts, 117, 118, 120
  forward stroke, 117–123
  key position, 119, 123
  rail tracks, 119
  technique, 116–124
  what hand to use, 116, 117
  when to use, 116

energy ratio, defined, 242
England, vi, 156, 162, 171
  Bray, the River, 47, 117
  Taw, the River, 47
  Torridge, the River, 47, 88, 224

Falkus, Hugh, 12
feed, defined, 242
flex
  basics of, 2–4
  defined, 243
  forward stroke and, 12
fly casting basics
  acceleration, 4–5
  flex, 2–4
  leverage, 3
  load, 2–6
  loop, 5–7
fly lines
  D loop and, 238
  overview of, 236
  profile of, 236–237, 243
  skagit, 237–239, 243
  weight of, 237–239
forward spey. *See* switch cast
forward stroke, 10
  See also under individual casts
  ABCs of, 11–12, 192
  defined, 9, 242
  flex and, 12

haul/hauling
  Chinese, 206–207
  defined, 242
  double haul turbo, 228–230
  preparation for, 192–195
  single haul turbo, 225–227
  steps in, 196–203
  technique, 192–207, 225–232
  triple haul turbo, 231–232
  when to use, 192
head, defined, 242
Heineken casts, 188, 224
  defined, 171, 242
Henry's Fork, 155

Ireland, vi

Kaufmann Spey Days, 208
key position, defined, 11, 20
  See also under individual casts
Kreh, Lefty, 162

leaders
  See also under individual casts
  casting style/requirements and, 241
  fishing applications and, 241
  overview of, 240
left bank, defined, 242
leverage, 3

lines. *See* fly lines
line stick, defined, 24
   See also under individual casts
load
   basics of, 2–6
   defined, 243
Loomis, 234
loop
   See also D loop
   control, slack-line casts and, 155–156, 160
   defined, 5–7, 242

mend, defined, 149, 150, 242
   See also aerial mend
McCune, Mike, 208, 213, 214
modern spey. *See* single spey, modern
Murray, Andy, 22

negative curve cast, defined, 242
New Zealand, 222

O'Donnell, Scott, 208, 213, 214
overhead cast, 8, 12, 18, 116, 132, 144, 145,
    149, 228
   alternatives, 20, 28, 47
   basics of, 2–7
   defined, 242
   side cast compared to, 126, 128–131, 134

parachute cast
   defined, 242
   technique, 157–160, 188
pick-up-and-lay-down cast, 8
piled (crumpled) anchor, defined, 242
pirouette, defined, 242
point P, defined, 24, 242
   See also under individual casts
poke
   defined, 217, 243
   technique, 217–222, 243
positive curve cast, defined, 243
power ratio, defined, 243
profile, of fly line, 236–237, 243

rail tracks, defined, 22, 243
   See also under individual casts
Rajeff, Steve, 234
reach cast, 149, 180
   defined, 144, 243
   fault finding, 147–148
   forward stroke, 144–146
   single spey with, 186–187
   technique, 144–148
   when to use, 144
right bank, defined, 243
RIO, 236, 237
Robinson, Eddie, 206
rod flex. *See* flex
rod load. *See* load
rods
   overview of, 234
   switch, 235

roll cast, 163, 167, 168, 171, 172, 225, 238
   See also double roll cast; roll cast with
    side cut
   backstroke (D-loop stroke), 18, 20, 25, 27,
    29, 31
   anchor, 24
   defined, 243
   D loop, 20–21, 24, 25, 27, 29, 31, 32, 35,
    36
   fault finding, 26–27
   forward stroke, 22–23, 25–27, 28, 30, 31,
    34, 36
   key position, 18, 20, 24, 29–31
   line stick, 24–25
   point P, 24–25
   rail tracks, 22–23, 26
   rod tip wiggle, 30–31
   shooting line on backstroke (D-loop
    stroke), 29
   shooting line on forward stroke, 28
   technique, 18–31
   when to use, 18, 20
roll cast with side cut, 171, 172, 175, 178
   acceleration, 164–166, 169, 170
   backstroke (D-loop stroke), 162–163, 167
   defined, 243
   D loop, 162, 163, 166–169, 175
   fault finding, 168
   forward stroke, 164–170
   key position, 162, 168
   line stick, 169
   rail tracks, 167
   technique, 162–170
   when to use, 162, 167
Roush, Marlin, 236
running line, defined, 243

Sage, 131, 234, 235
Scotland, vi
   Spey, the River, 47
scrub stroke, defined, 9, 243
   See also under individual casts
shepherd's crook cast, 144, 180
   defined, 243
   fault finding, 142–143
   leader rig for, 136–137, 142
   single spey with, 184–185
   technique, 135–143
   what hand to use, 138, 140, 141
   when to use, 135
shooting line
   defined, 243
   on backstroke (D-loop stroke) of roll cast,
    29
   on forward stroke of roll cast, 28
side cast, 8, 116–118, 136, 140, 141, 162,
    168, 171, 178
   acceleration, 130
   backstroke (D-loop stroke), 126,
    129, 130, 133
   defined, 243
   fault finding, 133–134

forward stroke, 126, 129, 130, 132, 133
   overhead cast compared to, 126, 128–131,
    134
   presentation, 130–132
   technique, 126–134
   what hand to use, 129
   when to use, 126–127
side cut, defined, 243
   See also roll cast with side cut; spey casts
    with side cut
side roll. *See* roll cast with side cut
side spey, defined, 243
side-to-side wiggle, 156–157, 160
Siem, Jerry, 131, 132, 234, 235, 241
single haul
   defined, 243
   turbo cast, 225–227
single spey, 87, 88, 100, 116–118, 120, 171,
    173, 180, 221
   aerial mend, with, 181–183
   anchor, 48
   defined, 243
   D loop, 48, 172
   forward stroke, 48, 175
   rail tracks, 48
   reach cast, with, 186–187
   shepherd's crook, with, 184–185
   slack-line cast, with, 188–190
   technique, 47–67
   what hand to use, 47
   when to use, 47
single spey, crude, 57
   backstroke (D-loop stroke), 52, 59–61
   defined, 242
   D loop, 50, 51, 56
   forward stroke, 50–52
   key position, 50–52
   rail tracks, 48, 50, 52
   technique, 48–52
single spey, modern
   acceleration, 61, 62, 63
   anchor, 61, 66
   backstroke (D-loop stroke), 59–61, 64–66
   bloody L, 66
   collision loop, 67
   defined, 242
   D loop, 63, 64, 66, 67
   fault finding, 65–67
   forward stroke, 60, 63, 64, 66, 67
   key position, 61, 62, 65
   line stick, 65
   rail tracks, 63, 66
   technique, 59–67
single spey, traditional, 64
   acceleration, 57–58
   anchor, 56
   backstroke (D-loop stroke), 54, 56–61
   defined, 243
   D loop, 56–58
   forward stroke, 54, 56–58
   key position, 53, 56
   technique, 53–58

single spey with aerial mend, 181–183
skagit line, 237–239, 243
Skagit River, 239
slack
    backstroke (D-loop stroke), 215–218, 222
    D loop, 215–223
    forward stroke, 220, 221, 223
    key position, 221
    overview of, 215
    poke, 217–222, 243
    setup stroke, 215, 219, 220
    technique, 216–223
slack-line casts, 180
    defined, 243
    forward stroke, 160
    loop control, 155–156, 160
    parachute cast, 157–160, 188, 242
    side-to-side wiggle, 156–157, 160
    single spey with, 188–190
    technique, 155–160
    when to use, 155
snake roll, 100, 116, 122, 171, 221, 222, 231
    acceleration, 89–91, 94, 95, 97
    anchor, 88, 93, 96, 99
    backstroke (D-loop stroke), 88–95, 97–99
    defined, 243
    D loop, 88–89, 91, 98, 99, 172
    fault finding, 97–99
    forward stroke, 92, 93, 96, 98, 99
    key position, 89, 92, 97
    rail tracks, 89, 97, 98
    reverse, 94, 96
    technique, 88–99
    what hand to use, 88, 94
    when to use, 88
snap C. *See* snap T
snap T, 171, 216, 231
    acceleration, 101, 103, 110
    anchor, 100, 104, 107, 108, 114, 115
    backstroke (D-loop stroke), 100, 101,
        104–108, 114, 115
    bloody L, 104, 108, 114, 115
    defined, 243
    D loop, 101, 106, 107, 172
    fault finding, 110–115
    forward stroke, 100, 101, 106–109, 111,
        113
    key position, 104, 106, 114, 115

other names for, 100
rail tracks, 101, 107, 111
setup stroke, 100–104, 110, 111, 114
technique, 100–115
what hand to use, 100, 109
when to use, 100
snap Z. *See* snap T
sneaky spey casts
    backstroke (D-loop stroke), 181, 184, 186
    D loop, 186, 188
    forward stroke, 182, 184–189
    leader rig for, 184
    rail tracks, 182
    single spey with aerial mend, 181–183
    single spey with reach cast, 186–187
    single spey with shepherd's crook,
        184–185
    single spey with slack-line cast, 188–190
    technique, 180–190
    when to use, 180
Spey, the River, 47
spey cast, defined, 243
Spey Casting (Gawesworth), 10
spey casts with side cut
    anchor, 178
    backstroke (D-loop stroke), 173, 175–179
    D loop, 171, 172, 175–179
    fault finding, 178–179
    forward stroke, 171, 173–179
    key position, 176–179
    line stick, 178
    point P, 176, 178
    technique, 171–179
    when to use, 171
splash and go, defined, 243
steeple cast
    defined, 243
    technique, 12
stick. *See* anchor
switch cast, 221, 225, 226, 228
    acceleration, 38–41, 46
    anchor, 38–41, 43–45
    backstroke (D-loop stroke), 37–41, 44, 45
    creeping, 45, 46
    defined, 243
    D loop, 35, 36, 39–41, 43
    fault finding, 44
    key position, 37–39, 41, 42, 45

line stick, 41, 44
forward stroke, 36, 38, 39, 41–46
point P, 42
rail tracks, 43
tailing loop, 46
technique, 35–46
when to use, 35
Sykomish River, 208

tackle
    fly lines, 236–239, 243
    leaders, 240–241
    rods, 234–235
tailing loop, defined, 243
    See also under individual casts
Taw, the River, 47
tempo, defined, 243
Thomas and Thomas, 234
timing, defined, 243
to-and-fro casts, defined, 8, 243
tongariro roll, 222, 243
Torridge, the River, 47, 88
    Jack's bay, 224
traditional spey. *See* single spey, traditional
turbo casts, 188, 222
    backstroke (D-loop stroke), 225, 226,
        228–232
    defined, 243
    D loop, 225, 226, 228–231
    double haul, 228–230
    forward stroke, 225–232
    key position, 232
    setup stroke, 231
    single haul, 225–227
    technique, 225–232
    triple haul, 231–232
    when to use, 224
turnover, defined, 243

United Kingdom, 4, 240
upstream wind, defined, 243

Wales, vi
Washington State
    Skagit River, 239
    Sykomish River, 208
waterborne anchor casts, defined, 9, 243
weight-forward, defined, 243